Gene A. Getz

JOSHUA

DEFEAT TO VICTORY

Regal
Books

A Division of GL Publications
Ventura, CA U.S.A.

Other good reading by Gene A. Getz:
Abraham: Trials and Triumphs
David: God's Man in Faith and Failure
   (with Study Guide)
Moses . . . Moments of Glory . . . Feet of Clay
   (with Study Guide)
The Measure of a Church
The Measure of a Family
The Measure of a Man
The Measure of a Woman (with Study Guide)

The foreign language publishing of all Regal books is under the direction of Gospel Literature International GLINT. GLINT provides financial and technical help for the adaptation, translation and publishing of books for millions of people worldwide. For information regarding translation, contact: GLINT, P.O. Box 6688, Ventura, California 93006.

Third Printing, 1983

Published by Regal Books
A Division of GL Publications
Ventura, California 93006
Printed in U.S.A.

Library of Congress Catalog Card No. 78-53358
ISBN 0-8307-0643-7

CONTENTS

WHY THIS STUDY?

When Joshua succeeded Moses as Leader in Israel, God clearly outlined how he could be successful, both in his personal life and in leading Israel as a corporate community. "This book of the law shall not depart from your mouth," God said, "But you shall meditate on it day and night to do according to all that is written in it." (Josh. 1:8).

This command in many respects represents an Old Testament declaration of what Paul shared with the Church in Rome in Romans 12:1,2. It is the basis for biblical renewal. Joshua took God's command seriously and consequently stands as a strong example for any Christian who desires to do the will of God. Personal renewal principles flow from his life and experience. Corporate renewal principles flow from his leadership experiences in Israel.

RENEWAL—A BIBLICAL PERSPECTIVE

Renewal is the essence of dynamic Christianity and the basis on which Christians, both in a corporate or "body" sense and as individual believers, can determine the will of God. Paul made this clear when he wrote to the Roman Christians—"be transformed by the *renewing of your mind*. Then" he continued "you will be able to test and prove what God's will is" (Rom. 12:2). Here Paul is talking about renewal in a corporate sense. In other words, Paul is asking these Christians as a *body* of believers, to develop the mind of Christ through corporate renewal.

Personal renewal will not happen as God intended it unless it happens in the context of corporate renewal. On the other hand, corporate renewal will not happen as God intended without personal renewal. Both are necessary.

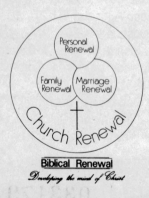

Biblical Renewal
Developing the mind of Christ

The larger circle represents "church renewal." This is the most comprehensive concept in the New Testament. However, every local church is made up of smaller self-contained, but interrelated units. The *family* in Scripture emerges as the "church in miniature." In turn, the family is made up of an even smaller social unit—*marriage*. The third inner circle represents *personal* renewal, which is inseparably linked to all of the other basic units. Marriage is made up of two separate individuals who become one. The family is made up of parents and children who are also to reflect the mind of Christ. And the church is made up of not only individual Christians, but couples and families.

Though all of these social units are interrelated, biblical renewal can begin within any specific social unit. But wherever it begins—in the church, families, marriages or individuals—the process immediately touches all the other social units. And one thing is certain! All that God says is consistent and harmonious. He does not have one set of principles for the church and another set for the family, another for husbands and wives and another for individual Christians. For example, the principles God outlines for local church elders, fathers and husbands regarding their role as leaders are interrelated and consistent. If they are not, we can be sure that we have not interpreted God's plan accurately.

The books listed below are part of the Biblical Renewal Series by Gene Getz designed to provide supportive help in moving toward renewal. They all fit into one of the circles described above and will provoke thought, provide interaction and tangible steps toward growth.

ONE ANOTHER SERIES	PERSONALITY SERIES	THE MEASURE OF SERIES
Building Up One Another	*Abraham*	*Measure of a . . .*
	David	*Church*
Encouraging One Another	*Joseph*	*Family*
	Joshua	*Man*
Loving One Another	*Moses*	*Marriage*
	Nehemiah	*Woman*
		Christian—Philippians
		Christian—Titus
		Christian—James 1

Sharpening the Focus of the Church presents an overall perspective for Church Renewal. All of these books are available from your bookstore.

ACKNOWLEDGMENT

I would like to express my gratitude to Dr. Kenneth Barker, professor of Semitic Languages and Old Testament Exegesis at Dallas Theological Seminary, who first read this manuscript and offered some very helpful suggestions as well as personal encouragement. Dr. Barker critiqued the first book in this personality series— *Moses ... Moments of Glory ... Feet of Clay*—and his positive response encouraged me to go on to do Abraham, David, and now Joshua.

INTRODUCTION

JOSHUA: DEFEAT TO VICTORY

One of the most exciting ways to learn practical truths from God's Word is to study prominent Bible characters —particularly Old Testament leaders. Joshua is one of those people. Perhaps more than any other Old Testament person, Joshua exemplifies for every Christian *positive* examples in how to live the Christian life. He stands out on the pages of the Old Testament as a man who, though he certainly made mistakes, very *consistently* obeyed God and walked in His will.

Most of what we learn is recorded in the book that bears his name—the sixth book in the Old Testament.[1] And though the *man*, Joshua, is the focus of our study, there are many additional lessons that we can learn from the larger context of his life and his relationship with others, including the children of Israel, the Canaanites and the unique individuals who were closely identified with him in the conquest of the land.

What can a twentieth-century Christian living in a vastly different culture learn from a man like Joshua? Just about everything we need to know to live a victorious Christian life. For example, Joshua teaches us that:

• God understands our human weaknesses—our fears, our anxieties, our feelings of inadequacy.

• God, our authority, will give us security in the midst of fear and stress.

• God wants all people to be saved from their sins and He continues to reach out to lost humanity.

• God honors true faith but He does not expect His children to operate on "blind" faith.

• God honors His children who honor Him.

• When the home ceases to reflect God's values, it takes only one generation for spiritual degeneration to take place.

• As twentieth-century Christians, we need "remembrances" lest we forget what God has done for us.

• God can take even our mistakes and turn them into positive results.

• We must take time on a consistent basis to maintain perspective on God's will for our lives.

• True love for God is the essence of Christian living.

• Doing the will of God involves a personal choice—an act of the will.

These are some of the dynamic and practical lessons we can learn from this study. But to understand and apply these truths in our daily lives, we need to take a look at Joshua's life and ministry—an exciting study.

Note

1. Most conservative Christian and Jewish Bible scholars believe that Joshua, the *man*, was the primary author of Joshua, the *book*. It is true there are sections he could not have written (such as the record of his death) but there is general agreement that we should credit Joshua with the substantial authorship of the book that bears his name.

JOSHUA'S PREPARATION

The Historical and Geographical Setting
Joshua's Childhood and Youth
Joshua's Wilderness Experience
Joshua's Change of Name

As a Christian have you ever become impatient because God's timetable doesn't match yours—especially in giving you a position of respect and recognition among other members of Christ's body? As a young Christian, a number of years ago now, I remember facing that tension in my own life. Little did I realize then how much I had to learn. Now, years later, I am very aware of how immature I really was and, interestingly, after 25 years in the ministry, I'm also very aware of how much more there is yet to learn.

Joshua is a positive example of an Old Testament leader whose preparation for leadership in Israel took many years. He was not uncommon in this respect among biblical leaders. God was never in a hurry to give them positions of heavy responsibility; He was concerned that they be adequately prepared.

What is unique about Joshua in his early years is his open heart, his willingness to learn and his spirit of humility. Consequently, he learned his lessons well.

THE HISTORICAL AND GEOGRAPHICAL SETTING

Who was Joshua? Where was he born? What kind of person was he? Why did he become the successor to Moses? To answer these questions adequately we must look at the larger context of the Old Testament and the circumstances leading up to the opening events in the book of Joshua, where Joshua the man appears as the leader of Israel.

Though significant events are recorded in the first 11 chapters of the Bible, the main story of the Scriptures actually begins in Genesis 12 with the Abrahamic covenant or contract. God made a promise to Abraham (originally called Abram) that He was going to bless him with a *land*—a permanent dwelling place. Furthermore, God promised Abraham a *seed*—a heritage, a great nation of people. And most important, God promised this Old Testament saint that through him the whole world would be *blessed* (see Gen. 12:1-3). God was speaking regarding a future son of Abraham, God's eternal Son, Jesus Christ, who would be born in due time and become the Saviour for all men (see Gal. 3:6-9).

At that moment in history God looked down on sinful and lost humanity. Out of a pagan culture—the world had turned away from Him as the one true God—He chose Abraham, a man who lived in Ur of the Chaldeans, to be the channel through whom He would provide a Saviour. "Abraham," God said, "I want you to leave your land, and I want you to go into a land I will give you—a land you've never seen before."

Abraham responded to God's call and command. By

12

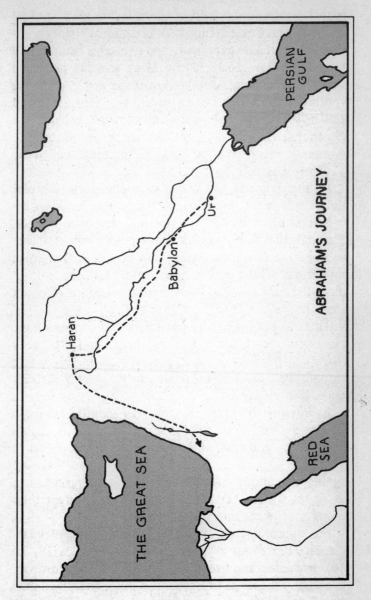

Map 1

faith he entered the land of Canaan (see map 1). And then a series of events followed. Looking at history compressed, Abraham eventually had two sons, Ishmael and Isaac (see Gen. 16:15; 21:2). Isaac was the promised seed, the true heir. And through Isaac, God's promises continued to unfold. Isaac also had two sons, Esau and Jacob (see Gen. 25:24-26). Jacob in turn became the channel God used to carry out His specific promise to Abraham. Jacob eventually had 12 sons, later called the 12 sons of Israel.

At this point in the Old Testament story, the plot thickens. Joseph, one of Jacob's sons, was hated by his brothers because he was favored by their father. Through an evil scheme, his brothers sold him as a slave to a band of Midianite traders and he was carried down into Egypt where he was again sold, this time to Potiphar, the captain of the bodyguard for the king of Egypt (see Gen. 37:28,36).

This was not the end for Joseph but just the beginning. He soon became a very successful man and eventually rose to a position of great prominence in Egypt. He actually became a ruler of all Egypt, serving directly under the Pharaoh.

Eventually, however, Joseph was reunited with his family. Through God's providential care, Jacob and all his children and grandchildren came to Egypt to escape a famine. Joseph forgave his brothers for their sin against him and arranged for them to have a place to live in Egypt where they could settle down and rear their families in peace and plenty.

For approximately 400 years the children of Israel (Jacob's name was changed to Israel—Gen. 32:28; 35: 10) prospered and grew into a large nation. However, eventually the kings of Egypt who knew Joseph all died (see Exod. 1:8), and one came to power who had a much different attitude toward this rapidly growing group of people. In fact, he felt threatened by the Hebrews' presence, and laid burdens on them they could hardly bear.

In God's timing He raised up a great leader named Moses who eventually led the children of Israel out of Egypt, across the Red Sea, through the wilderness and to the edge of the land God had promised to Abraham and to his descendants so many years before (see map 2, p.16.).

It's at this point that Joshua, the man we want to study, comes into prominence. Because Moses failed to obey God on one very important occasion, he was not allowed to enter the Promised Land. Rather, God designated Joshua as Moses' successor. And it was he who would lead the children of Israel into the land of promise.

JOSHUA'S CHILDHOOD AND YOUTH

Joshua was born in Egypt. His father and mother were slaves along with all the children of Israel who had become victims of Pharaoh—the "new king" who "arose over Egypt" and "did not know Joseph" (Exod. 1:8). As a young boy Joshua no doubt saw his father come home many nights from the fields, weary and exhausted from a toilsome day serving under the hard taskmasters of Egypt. Joshua was born many years after Pharaoh first became afraid of Israel's growth rate as a nation, but the persecution never subsided until the day Moses led them out of Egypt.

Joshua's early memories were not especially pleasant ones. Like any young Hebrew man, there were times when he could have lost his life. But in God's providence he survived. He particularly remembered one special night when his life was miraculously preserved. When Moses was preparing to lead the Hebrews out of Egypt, God sent a series of plagues upon that nation. The tenth plague involved the death of every firstborn

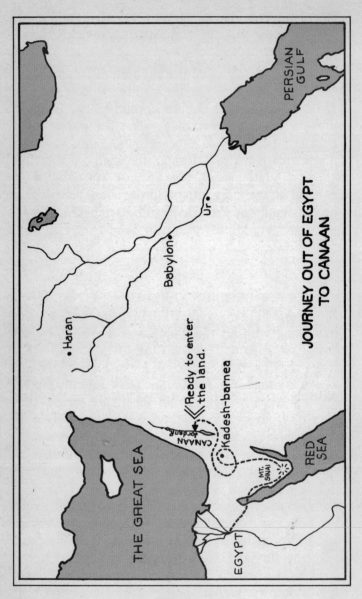

Map 2

in Egypt, including the animals, the Egyptians and the children of Israel. However, the Lord provided a way for Israelite parents to save the life of their eldest children. They were to prepare a Passover lamb and sprinkle its blood on the doorposts of their homes. And, said the Lord, "When I see the blood I will pass over you, and no plague will befall you to destroy you when I strike the land of Egypt" (Exod. 12:13).

Joshua evidently was the firstborn, the eldest son, in his family (see 1 Chron. 7:27). Neither he, nor any firstborn Israelite, could ever forget that night or the next morning. The mournful wailing of Egyptian parents filled the air as they discovered that every eldest child had been slain. But how wonderful to be among the living and among those who marched out of Egypt, following their great leader.

Already Moses must have become an ideal in Joshua's heart and mind. Joshua knew of Moses' great faith in God blended with courage as he saw him march into Pharaoh's court and pronounce judgment on Egypt. Joshua saw the results of that faith and courage as plague after plague came to pass—first, the waters of the Nile changed to blood, followed by the plague of frogs, gnats, insects, pestilence, boils, hail, locusts, great darkness and, finally, the death of every firstborn. And *then*, the greatest miracle yet. Joshua saw Moses stretch his rod over the Red Sea. He saw the waters part, allowing Israel to march across on dry ground. And then he saw Moses extend his rod once again over the waters, causing the sea to return to its place, destroying all the Egyptian warriors who followed the Israelites into the midst of the sea.

By this time in his life Joshua must have settled a very important issue—he *knew* and *believed* that the Lord God of Israel was indeed the one true God. And he also knew that Moses was God's appointed leader of Israel.

17

He soon became Moses' right hand man. In fact, this association may have begun even before they marched out of Egypt, for we read that Joshua, the son of Nun, was an "attendant of Moses from his youth" (Num. 11:28).

JOSHUA'S WILDERNESS EXPERIENCE

Moses soon developed unusual confidence in his young attendant. This is obvious from several significant events during the wilderness journey from Egypt to Canaan.

War with Amalek (Exod. 17:8-16)

Once on the way to the Promised Land Moses not only faced the threat of Israel's unbelief and desire to return to their pagan environment, but also the various enemies of Israel who resented their intrusion into their territory. Such was Amalek who attacked the Israelites at Rephidim, the place where Moses struck the rock and brought forth water. At this juncture Moses turned to Joshua to be his military assistant and issued an order for him to lead a counterattack. Joshua obeyed and with God's supernatural assistance led Israel to their first military victory in the wilderness.

Unknown to Joshua at this time, this was one of his first experiences that would help prepare him to lead Israel against numerous foes in the land of Canaan. The most important lesson from that experience was that God was on Israel's side. If they would obey Him they would have success in taking the land. And as we'll see in future chapters, though Joshua needed reassurance from the Lord Himself, he never forgot that victory over Amalek.

The Mountaintop Experience (Exod. 24:13-18)

When Israel arrived in the wilderness of Sinai and

camped in front of the mountain, God first spoke directly to all the people. Later He wrote His laws on tablets of stone and commanded Moses to climb the mountain, approach His presence and receive them. Significantly, Moses took Joshua with him (see Exod. 24: 12,13). And even more significant, the other leaders in Israel were not allowed to join them. "Wait here for *us*," said Moses to the elders, "until *we* [Moses and Joshua] return to you" (Exod. 24:14).[1]

The exact details in this story are not clear. It is doubtful that Joshua was allowed to experience God's glory to the same degree as Moses, but it seems that he was given greater access to the Lord's presence than the others. He alone was allowed to continue on up the mountain. At what point he remained behind and Moses went on alone to receive the tablets, we do not know. But we *do know* that his exposure to God's presence was second only to Moses. Joshua was so overwhelmed with Moses' personal relationship with the Lord that at times he would not leave Moses' side. We read:

> *Thus the Lord used to speak to Moses face to face, just as a man speaks to his friend. When Moses returned to the camp, his servant Joshua, the son of Nun, a young man, would not depart from the tent* (Exod. 33:11).

These experiences, though Joshua and Moses did not know it at this time, were all designed by the Lord to prepare Joshua for his future leadership role with the Israelites. Had Joshua known then, he would have lost emotional and spiritual perspective. Just knowing he was going to eventually replace Moses would have been far more than he could have handled psychologically at this juncture in his life. And of course, had Moses known that he was going to fail God in such a way that he would not be able to lead Israel into the Promised Land, he would have been so disheartened and discouraged he could not have gone on. Only God knows our future, and in His timing He unveils His sovereign plan, which in some incomprehensible way is interrelated and interwoven with man's freedom. Moses' sin and failure was not predetermined by God, but Joshua's unique preparation was! Only an omniscient and sovereign God can design a plan like that!

His Experience as a Spy (Num. 13:1—14:10)

Joshua's greatest test as a leader in Israel came when he was appointed as one of 12 spies to enter Canaan to survey the land. When they returned, only Joshua and Caleb were positive about entering Canaan as God said they should. The others were frightened by what they had seen—fortified cities and giant warriors—and they instilled this same fear in all Israel. Consequently, the whole nation rebelled against Moses and Aaron.

It was at this point that Joshua's spiritual qualities emerged as never before. He, along with Caleb, dared to confront all the congregation of the sons of Israel, saying:

> The land which we passed through to spy out is an exceedingly good land. If the Lord is pleased with us, then He will bring us into this land, and give it to us—a land which flows with milk and honey. Only do not rebel against the Lord; and do not fear the people of the land, for they shall be our prey. Their protection has been removed from them, and the Lord is with us; do not fear them (Num. 14:7-9).

Unfortunately the children of Israel would not listen. In fact, they rose up against Joshua and Caleb and tried to stone them. And at that moment God intervened and pronounced judgment on Israel. Because of their rebellion they had to wander in the wilderness for 40 years until all of that adult generation died. None of them could enter Canaan—except Joshua and Caleb. And of course, still unknown to Joshua, he would be the one who would lead the new generation across Jordan.

Joshua's experience as a spy taught him another very important lesson in the wilderness school. This was just another course God designed to prepare him for his future responsibilities. From God's perspective Joshua passed the test, and in another 40 years he would be ready to lead Israel into Canaan.

JOSHUA'S CHANGE OF NAME

There's one other important fact that must be mentioned concerning Joshua's preparation. Originally, his name was Hoshea (or Oshea, see Num. 13:8). Eventually Moses changed his name to Joshua (see Num. 13:16).

Why this change? The reason seems to be inherent in the names themselves as well as in the process God took Joshua through to prepare him for his future task. *Hoshea* means "salvation," but *Joshua* means "the *Lord* is salvation." It is true that Joshua would be God's human instrument to lead Israel into Canaan. In that sense he would be a means of salvation for God's chosen people. Though the Lord would definitely use what Joshua had learned at Moses' side—in Egypt, in the war against Amalek, on Mount Sinai, in his frightening encounter with Israel as one of the spies—yet it was God who would indeed lead Israel into Canaan. It was He who would roll back the waters of Jordan, cause the walls of Jericho to fall down, and defeat the people of Ai. It was God who would defeat all the giants in Canaan. Thus God changed Hoshea's name to Joshua to illustrate that He and He alone was Israel's salvation. And how well Joshua learned that lesson. In God's time he would be ready to allow the Lord to use his abilities and skills and *all* that he had learned during his years of preparation.

LESSONS FOR TODAY

There are several significant lessons that emerge from this introductory look at Joshua's preparation.

First, *it takes time to become prepared for any leadership responsibility.* Joshua's prominence in Israel came only after many years of faithfulness, both to the Lord and His commandments, as well as to Moses, God's appointed leader. Joshua proved himself worthy of trust.

Many Christians today want to bypass the process of demonstrating faithfulness over a period of time. Our tendency is to desire instant recognition, instant prominence, instant responsibility in fulfilling important leadership roles in the Body of Christ.

This is not God's plan. This is why Paul instructed Timothy to *not be hasty* in the laying on of hands (see 1 Tim. 5:22); in other words, be cautious in the appointment of spiritual leaders. Earlier Paul had charged Timothy to make sure that those desiring spiritual leadership in the church had a good reputation, were morally pure, that they demonstrated a well-ordered philosophy of life, that they were self-disciplined, had respect and credibility among others, that they were unselfish in the use of what God had given them, that they were not in bondage to fleshly appetites, that they were sensitive, non-defensive, kind, gentle and that they were able to function properly in their own families (see 1 Tim. 3:1-7). Finally, Paul stated that a Christian who is given heavy responsibility must not be a new Christian, primarily because of the temptation toward pride.

Second, *there is a unique balance between dependence on God and confidence in oneself.* It is true that God was going to use Joshua *the man* as a means to achieve His goals. But Joshua knew and so did Moses that it was in reality God Himself who would guide and direct Israel. It was *His power* that separated the waters of Jordan, *His strength* that caused the walls of Jericho to collapse,

His wisdom that enabled Joshua to strategize against the enemies of Israel.

This is a divine mystery. God does use men and women—our faithfulness, our commitment, our human abilities. But in reality, without Him we can do nothing that is worthwhile in His sight.

Third, *we must begin to serve God now in order to be prepared for future responsibility.* Though it takes time to become prepared to handle heavy leadership responsibility, that time should be spent faithfully serving God in less demanding roles and learning from more mature and experienced leaders. This was Joshua's strength. Moses was his example, his model and his teacher. And note! He served faithfully without even knowing that someday he would take over Moses' responsibility. This implies another reason why God chose him. Not only did he learn his lesson well but his motives were pure.

LIFE RESPONSE

This life response and the ones to follow are designed to help you personalize the lessons we will be learning from Joshua's life and experiences. Think carefully and seriously at this point. Unless you take this final step you'll miss what God intended when He recorded these Old Testament stories for us.

1. What about your life? Where are you in the process of demonstrating your commitment both to God and to other members of Christ's Body? Have you been faithful in the long haul? Do you realize that it often takes many faithful years of experience to be ready for God to entrust you with a heavy leadership responsibility?

NOTE: The amount of time involved in Joshua's preparation is not the important point in the story. In fact, there's no way to absolutize regarding the amount of time involved in a person's preparation to serve the Lord. Sometimes God shortcuts this process considerably. But the important point is that it *does* take time and it means faithfully fulfilling the tasks God gives us along the way. Success at one level prepares us for success at another level. It is only as we pass these tests that God entrusts us with more responsibility.

2. Even though men can build great kingdoms, achieve great goals, and even change the direction of history—seemingly without acknowledging God at all, it is only those who rely on God and know that all they have is from God who achieve goals that really make a difference in the light of eternity.

What about you? Are you concerned about the here and now—your immediate success, your reputation, your material accomplishments? If you are, you'll probably be successful by the world's standards. But in God's eyes you may be achieving absolutely nothing. Remember the words of Jesus, "But seek first His kingdom, and His righteousness; and all these things shall be added to you" (Matt. 6:33). This was Joshua's experience. And at the end of his life God surely said, "Well done, good and faithful slave" (Matt. 25:21). The greatest tribute to Joshua's ministry is recorded at the end of his life: "And Israel served the Lord all the days of Joshua and all the days of the elders who survived Joshua, and had known all the deeds of the Lord which He had done for Israel" (Josh. 24:31).

Write out an immediate goal for your life. Using the biblical guidelines just stated, what can you begin doing *now* to become better prepared to carry out God's work in the world? _____

_____

_____

_____

_____

_____

FOLLOW-UP PROJECT

Memorize the following verses:

> *Not that I have already obtained it, or have already become perfect, but I press on in order that I may lay hold of that for which also I was laid hold of by Christ Jesus. Brethren, I do not regard myself as having laid hold of it yet; but one thing I do: forgetting what lies behind and reaching forward to what lies ahead. I press on toward the goal for the prize of the upward call of God in Christ Jesus* (Phil. 3:12-14).

Note

1. Hereafter, all italicized words or words in bold type in Scripture quotations are inserted by the author for emphasis.

A
CALL
TO
COURAGE

God's Charge to Joshua (Josh. 1:1-6)
God's Conditions for Success (Josh. 1:7-9)
Joshua's Command to the People (Josh. 1:10-18)

I remember a very significant challenge several years ago in my own ministry. After teaching nearly 20 years (13 years in a Bible institute and 6 years in a theological seminary), I was asked by several families to lead them in launching a new church. It was to be a different kind of church than any I had ever been involved in. Though strongly committed to the Bible, forms would be much different from the average Bible-believing "traditional" church. Furthermore, we were committed to what we felt were several very important biblical principles—specifically, multiple leadership and total body function.

Frankly, though challenged, I was scared! Questions flooded my mind. What if we failed? Would people understand? What about those who would criticize us because they *didn't* understand?

In reality I felt just a little of what Joshua felt when

he was appointed leader of Israel—even though his leadership role was *many times* more threatening and demanding than mine. Though degree of responsibility varies greatly, often emotional response is similar. But God understands! He met Joshua's need—and He met my need in the same way.

How? For one thing, God blessed our efforts. Five years later, after launching that new church, we had ten congregations—four meeting in the original building and six branch churches. God *is* faithful.

GOD'S CHARGE TO JOSHUA (Josh. 1:1-6)

Following Moses' death Joshua faced one of the greatest challenges of his life. Though the role he found himself in as leader of Israel was no surprise, the reality of it all suddenly crushed in on him. Fear and anxiety gnawed at his total being. Threatening questions flooded his mind. How could he handle so great a responsibility? What if the children of Israel did not accept him as Moses' successor? Had they not just spent 30 days "weeping and mourning" over Moses' death (see Deut. 34:8)? What if he failed? What if there were national rebellion?

These were normal questions—especially in Joshua's circumstances. And God understood his dilemma, but God never gives a person a task without giving the resources, help and guidelines to carry out the responsibility. This truth is dramatically illustrated in God's words to Joshua in the introductory verses of chapter 1. These are words of *reassurance*. Previously the Lord had spoken *directly to Moses*. Now He speaks *directly to Joshua*. The key statements are: "Just as I spoke to Moses" and "Just as I have been with Moses, I will be with you" (1:3,5).

God understood Joshua's human weaknesses at this moment in his life. This new leader in Israel was frightened by the tremendous responsibility that had suddenly fallen on his shoulders. Even though God had prepared him ahead of time, the reality of the situation was awesome. Consequently, God charged Joshua to "be strong and courageous"—a phrase that appears four times in this introductory chapter (vv. 6,7,9,18).

Joshua's fears are understandable. After all, he had been chosen to follow in the footsteps of one of God's greatest leaders of all time, if not *the* greatest leader. And even though Joshua had proven himself again and again and had been told on several occasions that he was going to take over Moses' responsibility, when the moment finally arrived it was an overwhelming experience.

This of course was not an unpredictable response, particularly for a man who really understood the implications that lay ahead of him. Calvin once noted: "Even some of the bravest men, although fully prepared beforehand, either stand still or hesitate when the thing needs to be done."

Joshua was a brave man! There was no doubt about this. Had he not served as a successful military leader during the wilderness journey? Wasn't he one of the two spies (out of the 12) who had been positive about entering and conquering the land 40 years earlier even though humanly speaking it looked impossible?

And Joshua had been prepared beforehand. Earlier Moses informed the children of Israel that Joshua would lead them into the Promised Land. And in the presence of all Israel he charged Joshua:

> **Be strong and courageous,** *for you shall go with this people into the land . . . And the Lord is the one who goes ahead of you; He will be with you. He will not fail you or forsake you. Do not fear, or be dismayed* (Deut. 31:7,8).

And just before his death, Moses "laid his hands" on Joshua, commissioning him for this new task—again in the presence of all the sons of Israel (see Deut. 34:9).

But even with his obvious bravery and the preparation he had for the task, when the time finally arrived to take over the responsibility, Joshua was suddenly overtaken with fear. He was scared! And again, anyone with an understanding of the dynamics involved should be able to identify with Joshua's predicament. How would you feel about replacing a leader who God had declared could not be replaced? In position, yes! In quality, no! The Scriptures themselves declare: "Since then no prophet has risen in Israel like Moses, whom the Lord knew face to face" (Deut. 34:10). Though spoken from the perspective of history, Joshua obviously knew in his heart that there would never be another man like Moses.

Think for a moment! Suppose the board of directors of a large company selected you to be the next president. But as they appointed you they informed you that the late president was irreplaceable from the standpoint of leadership ability. Furthermore, you knew by experience that what they said was true. You had worked side by side with the previous president. You knew his ability. There was no way you could measure up in every respect!

How would you feel at this moment? No matter how much the board of directors tried to reassure you of their confidence in you and that you could do the job, the reality of the previous man's track record would continue to hang over your head. And the fact that you could never quite measure up would probably threaten you every day you left for the office.

In many respects this, intensified many times, was Joshua's predicament. He no doubt had seen Moses march into Pharaoh's court and pronounce judgment on the Egyptians. He had walked by Moses' side as Moses boldly led the children of Israel toward the Red Sea. He had watched in amazement as Moses held out his rod and parted that sea. He had accompanied Moses up the mountain that was red with fire and loud with thunderings and perhaps watched this man communicating with God face to face. He had seen this great leader of Israel come down from the mountain with his face aglow with the glory of God. And throughout the wilderness wanderings, Joshua had looked on as God used Moses as a human instrument to bring water out of the rock, to sweeten the waters of Marah, and to feed the children of Israel with quail and manna from heaven. Yes, Joshua knew all these things and they would be threatening for any human being.

But perhaps more frightening to Joshua than Moses' great achievements were the times when Israel rejected Moses. How could he help but remember vividly the times the children of Israel rose up against Moses, even threatening to kill him when he would not allow them to return to Egypt. And how could he forget his own personal involvement when he returned from spying out the land of Canaan and dared to confront those who defied God and refused to go in and take the land immediately. There is no way that Joshua could forget the many, many occasions when the unbelief of Israel was almost unbelievable.

And now Moses was gone! Here stood Joshua with the tremendous responsibility of taking over the leadership of this great multitude of unpredictable people. It is no wonder that God spoke *directly* to Joshua, repeating almost verbatim the words He had spoken to Moses (see Deut. 11:24; 31:3-8). It is no wonder that He charged Joshua to "be strong and courageous," reminding him of His promise to give Israel the land that lay before them. God understood Joshua's human emotions. Thus, He reassured him that He would help him do the job—even though he was replacing one of His greatest servants.

31

But the Lord did more than reassure Joshua of His presence and power. He also spelled out very specifically the *conditions* for successfully taking the land. God left no "ands, ifs and buts" undefined.

GOD'S CONDITIONS FOR SUCCESS (Josh. 1:7-9)

Five direct commands—all similar—stand out boldly as God's conditions for successfully taking the land of Canaan:

First, "Be careful to do according to *all the law*" (1:7a);

Second, "Do not turn from it to the right or to the left" (1:7b);

Third, "This book of the law shall not depart from your mouth" (1:8a);

Fourth, "You shall meditate on it day and night" (1:8b);

Fifth, "Be careful to do according to all that is written in it" (1:8c).

If you do these things, God said, *then* you will "have success wherever you go . . . *then* you will make your way prosperous" (1:7,8). In essence, what was the primary challenge Joshua faced? *First, he must make sure that he, Joshua, knew and understood the law that God had already given to Moses.* And there was only one way to achieve this goal. He must review it regularly and consistently—meditating "on it day and night."

Second, he must practice the law of God in his own personal and public life—not turning "from it to the right or to the left." There is no way he could lead Israel into obedience to God without exemplifying that obedience himself.

Third, and perhaps most important, he must boldly and with confidence communicate God's Word to the children of Israel. The law of God must not depart from his mouth.

Note, too, that all of these commands are stated in the context of being "strong and courageous." Two more times—within the space of these verses—God charged Joshua to overcome his fear. Becoming even more specific, the Lord said: "Do not *tremble* or be dismayed." In other words he was not to back away from his responsibility. He must not fear the children of Israel. He must not allow himself to become intimidated. He was to be strong like Moses. He was to speak not in his own strength but with the very authority of the Lord God of Israel.

Israel's success in taking the land was *conditioned* on their *obedience* to the Word of God. But, you say, wasn't the land promised to Israel unconditionally? What about God's promise to Abraham that we looked at in the previous chapter? How can you have *conditions* attached to an *unconditional* promise?

At this point the Scriptures may sound contradictory but they are not—if you indeed understand God's total program for Israel. First, you must realize that God's promise of the land of Israel *is* unconditional. And, not only is it unconditional, it is also *literal*.

Some Christians try to spiritualize this truth. Personally, I have difficulty spiritualizing "dirt" and "distance." Remember? Abraham was to *walk* up and down the land—on literal soil (Gen. 13:17). He was told by the Lord to *look* north and south and east and west, "for all the land that you see, I will give it to you and to your descendants forever" (Gen. 13:14,15). These were literal promises to Abraham and his children.

Many people who read about Israel in the Scriptures miss an important principle that resolves what may appear to be a contradiction. The principle is this: The ownership of the land of Israel *is* unconditional. It belongs to the children of Israel and eventually they will have it—*all of it!* However, they will not possess it totally and enjoy it until they are totally obedient to God.

This unconditional promise to Israel still stands. The conditions are still a reality. And one of these days, they'll have it—lock, stock and barrel. And God will do it. He will gather Israel from all nations and bring them into their own land. He will "sprinkle clean water" on them. He will give them "a new heart and put a new spirit within" them. This is what God meant when He revealed His will to Israel through Ezekiel the prophet:

> *I will put My Spirit within you and cause you to walk in My statutes, and you will be careful to observe My ordinances. And you will live in the land that I gave to your forefathers; so you will be My people, and I will be your God* (Ezek. 36:27,28).

As we'll see in the following chapters, Joshua cannot be faulted for his role in Israel's history. Under his leadership they had victory after victory and eventually experienced rest in the land. God was true to His promise of success. As long as Israel met His conditions, they were victorious. As long as they obeyed His Word as it was spelled out in Joshua 1:7-9, they had success wherever they went.

Consequently, we read in the last chapter of the book of Joshua:

> *And Israel served the Lord **all the days of Joshua** and all the days of the elders who survived Joshua, and had known all the deeds of the Lord which He had done for Israel* (Josh. 24:31).

Joshua was encouraged and strengthened by God's direct revelation. He wasted no time responding to God's charge and conditions. Immediately he called together the officers and leaders of the people and gave them a command.

JOSHUA'S COMMAND TO THE PEOPLE
(Josh. 1:10-18)

Joshua's command to the people of Israel can be divided into two sections. First, he spoke to *all* of the children of Israel (1:10,11). They were to get ready to move. They were going over Jordan to take the land.

Second, he spoke specifically to the Reubenites, the Gadites and the half-tribe of Manasseh. No doubt they were quite curious as to where they fit into the total scheme of things. To understand their questions, you need to understand several events that took place under Moses' leadership.

Israel had captured a parcel of land on this side of Jordan that was promised to the tribes of Reuben, Gad and the half-tribe of Manasseh. But the promise was given by Moses on one condition. The men from these tribes who were capable of being warriors were to pass over Jordan with the rest of Israel and help conquer the land of Canaan. When the job was finished, they could permanently return to the other side of Jordan and settle into the land Moses had promised them (see Deut. 3:8-19). These tribes agreed to Moses' condition as Joshua repeated it (see Josh. 1:16-18). They responded to Joshua's command willingly and with eagerness, "Just as we obeyed Moses in all things, so we will obey you; . . . only be *strong and courageous*" (1:17,18).

This response on the part of Israel was the reassurance Joshua needed. From this point on he was indeed their leader. There was no question, no doubt, no hesitancy. His fears and trembling turned into boldness, a steady hand and a quick stride that demonstrated an attitude of self-confidence blended with an unusual faith in God.

LESSONS FOR TODAY

There is one major point at which Joshua's experience

35

touches every one of our lives as twentieth-century Christians. We too must "be strong and courageous" no matter what our leadership responsibility and our position in life. As parents, church leaders, members of Christ's Body carrying out His work in this world, we can face our responsibility with confidence and assurance. And the basis of that security lies not in ourselves, but in the assurance that the same help that was available to Joshua is available to us.

First, God understands our human weaknesses—our fears, our anxieties, our feelings of inadequacy. God understood Joshua's emotional problems. Consequently, He moved quickly to reassure him and to help him rise above these frustrating circumstances.

God also understands *our* humanness. He made us. He knows us. He sympathizes with us. There is no struggle with which He does not identify. He does not stand over us ready to condemn us in moments of weakness. Rather, He is reaching out to help us, to reassure us—just as He did for Joshua! In fact, His great act of love in reaching out to us and sending Jesus Christ makes this truth possible on an ongoing basis. Consider the wonderful reality described in the Hebrews letter:

> *Since then we have a great high priest who has passed through the heavens, Jesus the Son of God, let us hold fast our confession. For we do not have a high priest who cannot sympathize with our weaknesses, but one who has been tempted in all things as we are, yet without sin. Let us therefore draw near with confidence to the throne of grace, that we may receive mercy and may find grace to help in time of need* (Heb. 4:14-16).

Second, our authority is based on the Word of God. The Lord dealt with Joshua's fear by reviewing for him His previous promises to Israel regarding the land of

36

Canaan. Furthermore, He charged Joshua to become thoroughly familiar with His law, to be sure to apply it to his own life personally and then to clearly and consistently communicate it to *all* the children of Israel.

Paul repeated the same basic instructions to Timothy, a young spiritual leader who oftentimes experienced fear in carrying out his pastoral responsibility. Very early in Paul's second letter to Timothy, he stated: "For God has not given us a spirit of *timidity*, but of power and love and discipline" (2 Tim. 1:7). Later, in the same letter he wrote: "Be *strong* in the grace that is in Christ Jesus .... Be diligent to present yourself approved to God as a workman who does not need to be ashamed, *handling accurately the word of truth*" (2 Tim. 2:1,15). And still later, Paul wrote: "I solemnly *charge*: ... Preach the word; be ready in season and out of season; reprove, rebuke, exhort, with great patience and instruction" (2 Tim. 4:1,2).

Third, obedience brings blessing. Martin Luther once said that "he who walks according to God's Word acts wisely and happily, but he who goes according to his own head acts unwisely and to no profit."

This simple but profound statement reflects a major lesson in the first chapter of Joshua. God shared with this new leader of Israel a very important secret to successful spiritual living and leadership—*obedience to His Word brings blessing.*

Rest assured that this is an ongoing promise throughout Scripture and applicable to all believers. And where it is not stated specifically, it is assumed. God honors obedience to His Word. Thus Paul wrote:

> *And do not be conformed to this world, but be transformed by the renewing of your mind, that you may prove what the will of God is, that which is good and acceptable and perfect* (Rom. 12:2).

Remember too that blessings from God are not only temporal but eternal. The most important reward for obedience to God's Word will be His "well done, thou good and faithful servant" (Matt. 25:21, *KJV*).

Fourth, God will never forsake us. "Be strong and courageous! Do not tremble or be dismayed, for *the Lord your God is with you wherever you go*" (Josh. 1:9). These must have been the most reassuring words that God spoke to Joshua. The Lord Himself promised to be his continual companion and divine resource.

Jesus made a very similar statement when He gave the Great Commission. "Lo," He promised, "I am with you always, even to the end of the age" (Matt. 28:20).

There is one who is forever faithful. As the author of the Hebrews letter reminds us, "He who promised *is faithful*" (Heb. 10:23). And the Old Testament prophet said it beautifully, "The Lord's lovingkindnesses indeed never cease, for His compassions never fail. They are new every morning; great is Thy faithfulness" (Lam. 3:22,23). And thus Christians have sung with confidence for many years William M. Runyan's great hymn of the faith:

> *Great is Thy faithfulness, Oh God my Father!*
> *There is no shadow of turning with Thee;*
> *Thou changest not, Thy compassions,*
> *   they fail not:*
> *As Thou hast been Thou forever wilt be.*

> *Pardon for sin and a peace that endureth,*
> *Thine own dear presence to cheer and to guide;*
> *Strength for today and bright hope for*
> *   tomorrow,*
> *Blessings all mine, with ten thousand beside!*

> *Great is Thy faithfulness! Great is Thy*
> *   faithfulness!*

Morning by morning new mercies I see;
All I have needed Thy hand hath provided;
Great is Thy faithfulness, Lord, unto me!

LIFE RESPONSE

Evaluate your own view of the responsibilities you have as a Christian. Are you fearful and anxious? Do you feel inadequate? Remember that you're not alone! Many of God's greatest leaders have experienced these feelings. But more important, God wants *you* to be "strong and courageous." And He has given you resources to achieve this goal. The following questions will help you to evaluate whether or not you are drawing adequately upon these resources:

1. Do I have a correct view of God's loving concern for me—that He wants to meet my need if I just let Him?

2. Do I take seriously the Word of God and its promises? Do I realize this is the greatest source of encouragement? Do I consult the Bible regularly? Do I meditate upon it? Do I obey it? Do I draw strength from it to carry out my responsibilities—since my authority is indeed based on God's authority?

3. Do I truly believe that obedience to God's Word will bring blessing, now and eternally?

4. Do I really believe that God is with me—that He has not forsaken me and He never will?

FOLLOW-UP PROJECT

Memorize Joshua 1:8:

This book of the law shall not depart from your mouth, but you shall meditate on it day and night, so that you may be careful to do according to all that is written in it; for then you will make your way prosperous, and then you will have success.

RAHAB THE HARLOT

Rahab's Test of Faith (Josh. 2:1-7)
Rahab's Statement of Faith (Josh. 2:8-11)
Rahab's Work of Faith (Josh. 2:12-21)
Rahab's Deliverance by Faith (Josh. 2:22-24; 6:22-25)

I was reared in a very religious subculture and attended a very pietistic church. In reality it was legalistic, which is not true biblical piety. But I did not know that then. In fact, I was controlled by spiritual pride and didn't realize it. Somehow I felt my religious background and heritage gave me a special corner on God's grace and love. In short, I felt I was better than other people who did not attend *my* church.

One day I suddenly awakened to the fact that there were other Christians, outside of my particular circle of friends, who were far more spiritual than I was. Though some of them had not had as much religious training as I, their faith was much stronger and more dynamic. They were more faithful in living up to the light they had.

41

In many respects this is what Israel discovered about Rahab the harlot, who lived in Jericho. Though she grew up and lived in a totally pagan and idolatrous culture, she responded in faith when she heard about the God of Israel. In certain respects she was more responsive spiritually than some of the Israelites. The Lord honored her faith and—what may be a surprise to some—included her in the Old Testament hall of faith in the New Testament.

What about *your* attitudes and behavior? How do you measure up to Rahab's faith?

RAHAB'S TEST OF FAITH (Josh. 2:1-7)

In studying the life of Joshua as he led the children of Israel into Canaan to conquer the land, some of the greatest spiritual lessons we can learn revolve around people who crossed his path. Such is the case with Rahab. No woman in all of Scripture stands out more boldly on the pages of Scripture as an object of God's redeeming grace. In fact, she is mentioned in Hebrews 11—the Old Testament hall of faith. Such greats as Noah, Abraham, Isaac, Jacob, Joseph and Moses are listed there. And all are commended for their faith. And somewhat surprising, here is where we find the name of "Rahab the harlot." Of her it is said: "By faith *Rahab the harlot* did not perish along with those who were disobedient, after she had welcomed the spies in peace" (Heb. 11:31).

How did a harlot find her way into the Old Testament hall of faith? The second chapter of Joshua makes the answer to this question very clear. Rahab lived in Jericho—an idolatrous and immoral Canaanite city. But in the midst of this den of iniquity, she came to know the one true God.

There seem to be two basic reasons why Joshua sent two spies into the land of Canaan. The first was a military reason. Thus Joshua issued the order: "Go, *view the land*, especially Jericho," (2:1), Israel's new leader wanted to know more about the land, particularly the attitudes of the Canaanites and what they knew about the battle plans of the children of Israel.

Interestingly, Joshua sent only two spies, perhaps a reflection of his own experience as a spy years earlier when he was sent as one of 12. Only he and Caleb returned with a positive report. The other 10 were negative and infected the whole nation of Israel with pessimistic attitudes, causing them to sin against God. They did not believe that God would enable them to conquer the land. Consequently God made them wander in the wilderness for 40 years.

Joshua was taking no chances this time. He was highly selective! Two would do—two men in whom he had confidence to give him an accurate report of the situation, who would not be intimidated by the enemy's military strength and their large "fortified cities" (Num. 13:28).

The second reason Joshua sent two spies into Canaan was providential, probably known at this moment only in the mind of God. This second reason, it seems, was far more important to the Lord than Joshua's military interests, for the bulk of chapter 2 is given over to the story.

A woman lived in Jericho who had come to believe in the living and true God. And there were others in Jericho who would yet respond in faith—her family.

The author of the book of Joshua wasted no time in focusing in on the primary subject of this chapter. Immediately we read: "So they went and came into the house of a harlot whose name was Rahab, and lodged there" (Josh. 2:1).

As soon as the spies entered Rahab's house she had more visitors—men from Jericho who had been sent by the king. Their mission was to search out the two spies from Israel.

How did the king in Jericho know so much? He knew they had entered Rahab's house. He knew they were men. He knew they were together and had not split up. He knew they were "sons of Israel." He also knew the exact arrival time—that very night. And he knew their purpose—"to search out the land" (Josh. 2:2).

From a human perspective there's only one answer to this question. Already the kings of Canaan had set up a tremendous security system. Evidently, their own spies were watching every move the children of Israel made. They must have known when the spies left the camp on the other side of Jordan; they must have seen them cross over the river and followed their every move. Obviously they knew when they entered the city of Jericho and they followed them directly to Rahab's house. All of this information was conveyed to the king of Jericho at regular intervals. When he learned that the spies had entered Rahab's house, he immediately ordered their capture.

This leads to another question. Why was the king so concerned about their capture when they entered Rahab's house? Why had he not issued this order earlier? Could it be that Rahab was already known in Jericho for her change of heart? Could it be that the men who had visited her regularly were already being confronted with what was beginning to happen in her life? As we'll note later, it appears that she had been warning the people of Jericho of impending doom. And perhaps the spies from Israel had also heard about Rahab's concerns and sensed they would be welcome there.

These questions and observations are of course speculative. But they're well within the realm of reality. When the king's men arrived at Rahab's to take the two spies into custody, she had already hidden the spies on her roof under stalks of flax—as if she already knew that her home would be searched. Why this concern? Why this eagerness to protect the sons of Israel? Why the willingness to take a chance on her own life should the spies be discovered? All of these questions point to one basic answer: Rahab had already changed her allegiance!

Rahab lied to the men of Jericho. She had grown up in a pagan city where the normal life-style was lying, cheating and all forms of immorality. She was a prostitute by profession. She had worshiped the false gods of Canaan; her knowledge of the one true God only recently had come into focus. But Rahab *was* responding to the light she had. And God honored her faith in spite of her sin and failure. She passed the test. She was literally willing to take a chance on her own life.

In many respects Rahab was already ahead of many of the children of Israel. Their light was far greater. They had experientially *seen* miracle after miracle; whereas Rahab had only *heard* about them. The children of Israel had received the law of God by means of direct revelation to Moses; whereas Rahab had only heard indirectly about God's will. Even with all this light, Israel turned their backs on God again and again, indulging in horrible sins. It appears that God was giving greater attention to Rahab's faith. Why? Because she was more faithful to the light she had—dim as it was. Compared to Israel, her faith was greater. And she proved it by risking her life for the people of God. In this case, God looked beyond her human weakness and saw where she was coming from, and where she was heading.

The degree of Rahab's faith is seen by her willingness to hide the spies in her home. She must have been fully aware of the king's surveillance system. Her risk was great. As we have seen, the king's system was so effective that his men followed the two spies' every move—

from the time they left camp until they entered Rahab's home. How easy it would be for the king's men to discover two men on a rooftop!

Why would they suddenly believe that Rahab the harlot was telling the truth when she told them the spies had left? Why didn't they search the house before running out into the darkness in search of the spies? There doesn't seem to be a satisfactory human answer to these questions. It was no doubt a miracle. God was honoring her faith. It would be no problem for God—the one who parted the Red Sea and destroyed the Egyptians—to turn these men away from Rahab's house and even cause them to believe a lie. You see, God can even turn evil into good. And only God—the God of Abraham, Isaac and Jacob *and Joseph* (see Gen. 50:20)—can do that!

Rahab's faith, weak as it was, was tested. And she passed the test. She dared to believe that this God she had heard about would protect her too. And God did not let her down!

RAHAB'S STATEMENT OF FAITH (Josh. 2:8-11)

Rahab's willingness to risk her life to protect the men of Israel is significant evidence that she was in the process of changing her way of life. But her statement of faith in verses 8 to 11 clearly reveals the simple theology that was guiding her behavior.

After the men of Jericho left to pursue the spies from Israel, "She came up to them on the roof" (2:8). Note the certainty with which she spoke to these men—"*I know,*" she said, "that the Lord *has given* you the land" (2:9). Rahab saw the fear of her own people in Jericho and of the other inhabitants of the land. She heard about the miracles God had performed for Israel—the parting of the Red Sea and the great victories over the Amorites on the other side of Jordan (see 2:9-11).

46

But there was a great difference between Rahab and the other Canaanites. She acted on what she knew. She acknowledged that God was the true God. Her statement of faith was very specific when she said: "For the Lord your God, He is God in heaven above and on earth beneath" (2:11).

Rahab's fellow Canaanites, who had the same knowledge as she, did not acknowledge the God of heaven. They would not respond to the light they had been given. And because of their unbelief they were heading for immediate and eternal destruction and separation from God. Consequently, the writer of Hebrews wrote:

> **By faith** *Rahab the harlot did not perish along with those who were disobedient, after she had welcomed the spies in peace* (Heb. 11:31).

RAHAB'S WORK OF FAITH (Josh. 2:12-21)

Already we've seen Rahab's faith tested. And we've seen her pass the test. Her faith was real! But the real test still lay ahead. Her substantial *work of faith* was yet to be demonstrated.

An Unselfish Request

If I had been Rahab, knowing what she knew and believing what she believed, my first temptation would be to ask the spies if I could leave with them. Rather than *telling* them where to hide (see 2:16), I'd have wanted to *show* them the hill country where they could hide (see 2:16).

Rahab might have faced this temptation. This was her golden opportunity to join the children of Israel before destruction and doom hit Jericho. But she did not take that opportunity. She overcame that temptation. If she wavered at all, it is not noticeable in the historical record, for her first request was not for herself but for

47

her household (see 2:12). "Spare my father and my mother and my brothers and my sisters, with all who belong to them," she pleaded (2:13).

The men of Israel responded favorably and proposed a plan. They told her to hang a "cord of scarlet thread" in her window and bring all of her relatives into her home. And when Israel marched on Jericho, all those in her home would be spared (see 2:18).

The Scarlet Rope

The scarlet rope or "cord" is very significant. It no doubt points to the fact that Rahab had already changed her life-style and entered a new vocation.

No, I'm not talking about *red* referring to the blood of Christ—although you may read this typology into the story if you wish. It *is* beautiful symbolism. But rather, I'm referring to the literal historical meaning that is associated with this "cord of scarlet thread."

To understand this meaning more clearly we need to back up in the story to the "stalks of flax which [Rahab] had laid in order on the roof" of her home (2:6). Gathering flax was a very laborious task. Industrious women of old would spend hours gathering these stalks to make cloth. In fact, the book of Proverbs describes one characteristic of a virtuous woman as one who "looks for wool and *flax*, and works with her hands in delight" (Prov. 31:13).

If Rahab had still been practicing her old profession, chances are she would not be spending time gathering flax, since prostitutes are not known for the time they spend doing regular work. And it's important to note that Rahab had gathered *enough* flax to cover up two grown men. Evidently she had been in the cloth business for some time.

But where does the red rope fit in? This, even more than the flax, points to a change of profession. When the ancients made dye they would boil it out of rocks. And since liquid dye was difficult to transport and store, they would put a piece of rope into the dye to absorb it. Cloth makers then would buy pieces of the rope to dye their clothes. While the cloth was boiling in water, they would drop a piece of the dyed rope in the container and the color would transfer from the rope to the fabric. Usually a very small piece of rope—six inches or so—would dye a large quantity of cloth.

This is an important point. Rahab had enough rope to hang all the way over the wall so the men could climb down. Furthermore, it's important to note that the wall may have been as high as 30 feet. For a cloth maker, that's a lot of rope! Evidently Rahab's cloth business was no minor operation. She may have changed her profession sometime before.[1]

RAHAB'S DELIVERANCE BY FAITH
(Josh. 2:22-24; 6:22-25)

When the spies returned to the camp of Israel, they reported to Joshua that the Canaanites were very frightened. "Surely," they said, "the Lord has given all the land into our hands" (2:24). But probably the most intriguing story they shared was their encounter with Rahab and how they had promised her deliverance when Israel attacked Jericho.

However, there was something the spies did not yet know. God was going to destroy the walls of Jericho—and *Rahab lived on the wall!* Can you imagine the consternation that must have gripped these men when God revealed His plan to the children of Israel.

As we'll see in a future chapter, the walls of Jericho *did* fall down (see Josh. 6:20)! But Rahab *was* saved, just as these men had promised.

But how did it all happen? What happened to her house when the walls fell down? There can be only one explanation: still left standing for all to see, Israel included, was one section of the wall with one lonely house—a house with a scarlet rope hanging from the window. Rahab and her entire family were saved. God honored her faith!

LESSONS FOR TODAY

First, God wants all people to be saved from their sins. One of the most appropriate ways to bridge the gap between this Old Testament story and our lives today is to look at a New Testament parallel. Joshua said, "Go, view the land, *especially* Jericho" (Josh. 2:1). Many years later, the apostle John wrote that Jesus "*had* to pass through Samaria" (John 4:4). There was a sense of predetermined urgency in both of these statements. And in both of these stories we encounter women of ill repute. Both responded to the light they had and both became immediate witnesses of their faith.

Perhaps the greatest lesson that jumps off the pages of Joshua chapter 2 and John chapter 4 is that God cares about *individuals*, particularly individuals who have fallen into a state of deep sin and degradation. Why else would He give so much space in the midst of divine history to record the conversion of two such people? God's desire is that all people know that Jesus Christ died for the sins of the world. There's no individual outside the sphere of His love and grace.

There's another intriguing fact in Scripture that points to this truth. If Rahab had become a believer, why then would God choose to record her name in the New Testament as "Rahab the harlot"? Was it not to demonstrate His grace? God is no respecter of persons. All men and women everywhere can call on the name of the Lord and be saved (see Rom. 10:13).

This of course is not a new phenomenon in Scripture. One of the apostles was called Simon the Zealot (see

50

Mark 3:18). Zealots were radical Jews, similar in function to radical groups in our own culture who are given to violent tactics to bring about reform in society. They were often involved with assault and killing. Obviously, Simon changed his profession after becoming a follower of Jesus Christ. And yet he retained his name—Simon the Zealot—additional evidence of the grace of God in calling such a man to be one of His choicest servants.

Rahab, then, entered Israel with a name of shame. But she was soon to become an outstanding woman. In fact, her name actually appears in the genealogy of Jesus Christ—the Saviour of the world (see Matt. 1:5).

Second, God honors true faith. Faith is not a static word. It's an action word. James wrote, "Faith, if it has no works, is dead" (Jas. 2:17). Rahab had an active faith. In that sense she was "justified by works" (Jas. 2:25), not that she was *saved* by works, but rather she *proved* her faith by her works. The quality of her faith stands out in at least four ways.

1. Rahab took God at His word. Her first words in Joshua 2:9 were, "I know." There was no doubt. She believed that the God of Israel was the one true God and that He alone could be trusted.

What about you? How strong is *your* faith? Do you believe in God and in His Son Jesus Christ with the same intensity as Rahab? Remember, your light is much greater than hers, as was Israel's. Is your faith commensurate with your knowledge?

2. Rahab's faith produced self-denial and a refusal to go along with the rest of the world. She gave up her former profession and became a maker of cloth. In receiving those messengers of God she denied everything her countrymen stood for. With this act of faith she renounced everything in her past. She was no longer a part of the world of Jericho. Her life was different and people noticed it.

51

Again, what about you? Does your faith in Jesus Christ really make a difference in the way you live? Are you willing to put your life and reputation on the line because of your commitment to God and to His system of values?

3. Rahab's faith caused her to be concerned for others and to seek them out. Rahab convinced her whole family to come to her house and stay there for the seven days the army of Israel circled the city. She had no way of knowing when the attack was going to come, but she must have communicated as if the walls were going to fall at any moment. She operated with a sense of urgency.

What about you? Do you really believe that people are lost without Christ, that final judgment is eventually coming? Obviously we can become neurotic and improperly obsessed about this matter, not trusting God to carry out His divine and sovereign plan. But on the other hand, we must blend human responsibility with His divine perspective. God has given us the task to share His message of grace with those who do not believe.

4. Rahab's faith caused her to be very bold in asking for God's help. Her theology was simple but her faith was great.

For some of us, our knowledge gets in the way of our faith. How unfortunate! The more we know *about* God, the more we should *believe* God. Let's not allow ourselves to get lost in a theological maze, trying to unravel all the ramifications of God's great plan, and miss His greatest desire for us—that we trust in Him with all our hearts and act on that faith!

LIFE RESPONSE
1. Do you really believe God truly cares about your spiritual welfare? Do you believe He will forgive your

sins no matter what you have done? If you have any doubts about this, think about Rahab! God *does* care about you! That's why He sent His only Son into this world to die for our sins. Receive Jesus Christ today as your Saviour and Lord!

2. As a Christian consider the following four areas in your life. Select one area that you feel is the weakest and needs the most attention. Decide on one specific way you can change that area of your life. For example, if you select number one, write out one area where you are not taking God at His word. Then pray and ask God to help you reach this goal.

• I do not really take God at His word and move into an active, believing, living life-style.

• There are areas in my life where I am needlessly going along with the world. I'm not willing by faith to break these old associations for fear of ridicule and persecution.

• I'm not actively witnessing for Christ, believing that judgment is actually coming someday.

• I'm not boldly approaching the throne of grace in faith, believing God for the seemingly impossible.

FOLLOW-UP PROJECT

Memorize Hebrews 11:6 for meditation and encouragement:

> *And without faith it is impossible to please Him, for he who comes to God must believe that He is, and that He is a rewarder of those who seek Him.*

Note

1. There are some who believe Rahab operated an inn. This is certainly a feasible interpretation. Perhaps she was both a cloth maker and an innkeeper.

CROSSING THE JORDAN

Joshua Moves Ahead by Faith (Josh. 3:1-6)
God Speaks to Joshua (Josh. 3:7,8)
Joshua Speaks to the People (Josh. 3:9-13)
The Children of Israel Cross the Jordan (Josh. 3:14-17)

Early in my Christian life I was confused about the subject of faith. Somehow I thought that faith involved a leap in the dark—a "blind faith" if you will. "If God says it, I believe it," I would often say.

Today I would still say, "If God says it, I believe it!" But there's a difference. I know now that I need not apologize or become defensive about faith in God's word as it is revealed in the Bible. I now understand that God has never asked people to believe in something that is not based on reality and upon substantial facts. This is the way it has *always* been, even in Old Testament days. When God asked Joshua to approach the Jordan River and to believe that the waters would roll back, Joshua's faith was based not only on God's direct statements to him personally, but upon previous experience, one of which was the similar, very dramatic parting of the Red Sea.

JOSHUA MOVES AHEAD BY FAITH (Josh. 3:1-6)

When Joshua's two spies returned from Jericho they were enthusiastic about entering the land of Canaan. *"Surely,"* they reported, "the Lord has given *all* the land into our hands, and *all* the inhabitants of the land, moreover, have melted away before us" (Josh. 2:24).

God had already reassured Joshua that the land was theirs (see 1:2-4). And Joshua believed what God had said (see 1:10,11). But the report from the two spies added a touch of reality that bolstered his faith. God knew what His servant needed. And though He had made it very clear that victory was already guaranteed if they met His conditions, yet the Lord allowed Joshua to accumulate some military evidence to make it easier to continue to actively believe God's promise.

Joshua's greatest test of faith, however, lay just ahead. Though the Canaanites who lived beyond Jordan appeared to be no obstacle, the children of Israel faced a raging river that separated them from the land. Spies or no spies, this problem was in many respects just as great as the one Moses faced when he stood on the shore of the Red Sea with no human means to get to the other side. Joshua, like Moses, took God at His word and trusted Him to do the impossible!

As we've seen from the story of Rahab, true faith and godly works go hand in hand. This truth is also illustrated dramatically in the life of Joshua. He wasted no time after he had received the positive report from his spies. He broke camp "early in the morning" and moved the whole company of Israelites close to the Jordan River (see map 3).

Can you imagine the questions that were going through the minds of the children of Israel? Ahead of

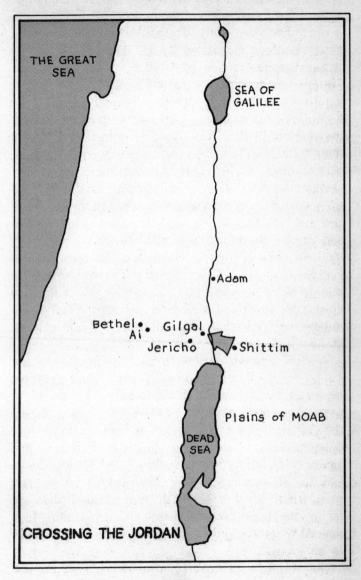

Map 3

them flowed a wide and rushing torrent of water. The Jordan River was at flood tide, as wide as a football field is long. The very word "Jordan" means "descender." The river drops approximately 1,000 feet as it makes its journey from the Sea of Galilee to the Dead Sea. Though this descent has created a natural current, during flood tide the speed increases to nearly 10 miles per hour. Humanly speaking, there was no possible way for the children of Israel to cross over with their children, their animals and their supplies. There were no bridges, no ferryboats, no helicopters! Just rushing water.

Remember, too, that the children of Israel who faced this present crisis represented a new generation. They had not seen the parting of the Red Sea. Only Joshua and Caleb were among those who crossed the sea on dry land. Because of their disobedience, the generation of people coming out of Egypt died in the wilderness during the 40-year wandering. This new generation had heard only reports of what God had done. Their minds must have been filled with ambivalence—a mixture of anticipation and fear. Would God act again?

At this juncture Joshua himself probably did not know specifically what God was going to do, except that he believed that the Lord would make it possible for them to cross the river. As he marched forward bearing the responsibility of thousands of lives, he must have bolstered his courage by repeating to himself again and again God's initial words to him after Moses' death. "Moses My servant is dead; now therefore arise, *cross this Jordan*" (Josh. 1:2). On the human side Joshua was facing the greatest test of his life. What if nothing happened? What would the people do? What would happen to his image?

But Joshua's faith overruled his fears. Furthermore, his faith was contagious. The Levitical priests led the way carrying the Ark of the Covenant, a small box, probably about four feet long, two and one-half feet wide, and about two and one-half feet high. It was overlaid with gold inside and out. The ark contained the tables of stone on which God Himself had written the law, as well as other symbols of God's leadership. When the people set up camp the ark was placed in the holy of holies in the Tabernacle (see Exod. 26:33).

Now the ark was being carried out ahead of Israel as they marched toward Jordan. And since the ark represented God's presence, the children of Israel sensed that God Himself was leading them right up to the edge of the river.

The depth of Joshua's faith is seen in his confident statement to the people: "Consecrate yourselves, for *tomorrow* the Lord will do wonders among you" (Josh. 3:5). The specifics seemingly were yet to be revealed, but Joshua believed that God would give those instructions when they were needed. And because God is faithful to His promises, He did just that!

GOD SPEAKS TO JOSHUA (Josh. 3:7,8)

It's very important to note that Joshua's work of faith was not based on *blind* faith—some inner thought or intuitive feeling. It was faith based on fact. God had spoken, not through some inner voice or existential experience, but through direct revelation. Joshua in some miraculous way *heard* the voice of God say, "I'm going to take you across Jordan," just as God had verified His presence with Israel on many occasions when Moses was leading them.

Yes, Joshua was moving ahead by faith, but it was faith based on God's direct revelation in verbal form as well as in a variety of other phenomenal events. God's presence with Israel was a fact of history.

And once again God was speaking directly to Joshua, and just at the right time.

This day I will begin to exalt you in the sight of all Israel, that they may know that just as I have been with Moses, I will be with you (Josh. 3:7).

This was a specific promise with a specific meaning. When God said to Joshua, "Just as I have been with Moses, I will be with you" (1:5; 3:7), He was referring to that great event many years before when Israel was being pursued by the Egyptian army. The Red Sea lay ahead and their enemies were coming up behind. It was then that God told Moses to stretch out his rod over the Red Sea. And the waters parted. It was then that Israel passed over on dry ground. And when they arrived safely on the other side, God instructed Moses to wave his rod over the sea once again. And the sea came together with great force, drowning all the Egyptians who followed.

Joshua understood clearly the meaning of this present promise. God's power was going to be with him as it was with Moses. He understood the significance of God's specific instructions to the priests. They were to walk into the waters of Jordan, carrying the ark. After proceeding a short distance into the river, they were to stand still and wait for another miracle.

In order to understand this maneuver, it's helpful to visualize what the Jordan River was like at flood tide. When conditions were normal, the Jordan flowed at a lower level. But when the snow began to melt in the mountains, the Jordan River overflowed its banks to a second level which was ordinarily covered with shrubs and other growth. When the priests stepped into the water with the ark, the river was probably at its highest point (see Josh. 3:15).

JOSHUA SPEAKS TO THE PEOPLE (Josh. 3:9-13)

God's instructions to Joshua regarding the crossing of

the Jordan were startling, but not unusual. Frequently, God would speak to Joshua and he would then be God's instrument to relay the Lord's message to the children of Israel. In fact, the Bible does not record many times when God spoke directly to a large group of people at the same time. He usually spoke to one or a few individuals—people He had especially selected to be His divine messengers.

At this time in the history of Israel Joshua was God's divine messenger to them. But notice what Joshua said: "Today you will begin to see God exalt *me* in your presence!"

Is this what Joshua said to the people? Not at all! It's what God said to Joshua, not what Joshua said to the people. Rather, Joshua said, "By this you shall know that the *living God is among you!*" (Josh. 3:10.)

By rights, Joshua could have repeated to Israel exactly what God had said to him. But he didn't. There was no hint of pride or arrogance! His concern was that God be honored and glorified in what was about to happen.

But think of the temptation Joshua must have faced. How easy it would have been to draw attention to himself and to attempt to build his own ego. And what greater opportunity to engage in a lot of self-glorification than when God Himself had spoken so specifically to Joshua about the fact that He would exalt him.

Joshua, primarily because of his feelings of insecurity, was vulnerable to this kind of temptation. Remember how threatened he was when he realized that Moses' mantle had fallen on his shoulders? He was so frightened he literally trembled. Fearful people are vulnerable to pride. They often overreact to praise and honor. Their temptation toward self-exaltation is often greater than it is in people who are basically secure.

Joshua, however, did not respond either with false humility or with pride. He had discovered security in

61

God's promises to him. He was able to rise above the temptation to glorify himself. He gave honor to the only One who could be given credit for the miracle that was about to take place.

Joshua's response was admirable, especially in view of the fact that he had been fearful and threatened by this great task. But his response represents the main reason why God chose to use Joshua in the first place. He knew He could trust him with this leadership role. He knew Joshua could handle the temptation that comes to every individual who is entrusted with great responsibility.

Understand, however, that God does use men—their talents and abilities. Joshua was such a leader. He had proven himself many times. He was a brilliant strategist. He had sent out the spies, he had thought through the issues, and he had communicated effectively to his leaders. But when it came to telling the children of Israel what God's plan was for him specifically, he completely bypassed the opportunity to exalt himself.

THE CHILDREN OF ISRAEL CROSS OVER JORDAN (Josh. 3:14-17)

The great event was about to happen! The priests stepped into the water of the Jordan River. Suddenly the rushing torrent began to back up—all the way to the city of Adam. What a fantastic sight this must have been! Some scholars believe the city of Adam was located as much as 30 miles back up the Jordan (see map 3).

Have you ever wondered why God backed the waters up so far? Think again! What do you suppose the Canaanite spies were thinking when this unbelievable phenomenon was taking place? And what do you think happened to their spirits when thousands of Israelites began to march across the Jordan on dry ground? No doubt this miracle could be *heard* and *seen* for miles around. In a matter of hours, every king on both sides of the Jordan was aware of what was happening.

With this miracle God was not only exalting Joshua in the eyes of the children of Israel. He was also demonstrating once again His power and majesty to the pagan world, to lost mankind, to men and women and children He loved and whom He wanted to turn to Him in faith and obedience. He was once again giving the inhabitants of Canaan another opportunity to repent of their sins and turn from their gods of wood and stone to worship Him, the living and true God. He was already in the process of saving Rahab and her family from destruction and judgment. And personally I believe He would have saved any other inhabitants in Canaan who would have turned to Him in faith. To warn people of coming judgment and then to relent when people repent is part of the very character and nature of God.

Take the Ninevites for instance. God chose Jonah to warn these people that He was going to destroy them because of their evil deeds. And eventually, after trying to run away from God's will, Jonah preached a message of doom in this great city. "Yet forty days and Nineveh will be overthrown" (Jon. 3:4). There were no "ifs or buts" in this message. Disaster was imminent.

But notice! The people of Nineveh listened to Jonah. They repented in sackcloth and ashes. And "when God saw their deeds, that they turned from their wicked way, then God relented concerning the calamity which He had declared He would bring upon them" (Jon. 3:10).

It is impossible to explain how a sovereign God who declares something is going to happen can actually change His mind. But when people repent, God relents! Inherent in God's nature is the ability to withdraw judgment when man turns to Him.

God had been issuing warning after warning to the Canaanites that doom was coming. From the Red Sea onward, with the miracles in the wilderness, with the 40 years' judgment upon Israel, and now with the parting of the Jordan, God was saying: Doom is coming! Repent! Turn from your wicked ways and your false gods and worship me!

And make no mistake about it! The Canaanites got the message. Rahab reported to the spies:

> *We have heard how the Lord dried up the water of the Red Sea before you when you came out of Egypt, and what you did to the two kings of the Amorites who were beyond Jordan . . . . And when we heard it, our hearts melted and no courage remained in any man any longer because of you* (Josh. 2:10,11).

The difference of course is that Rahab turned from her sin and false gods to worship the true God: "For the Lord your God," she said, "He is God in heaven above and on earth beneath" (2:11). But the vast majority of the Canaanites refused to give up their idolatry. Had they repented, had they listened to the voice of God through Israel, He would have turned away His wrath and with a heart of love welcomed them into the fold of security and protection. Jonah tells us this when he said:

> *For I knew that Thou art a gracious and compassionate God, slow to anger and abundant in lovingkindness, and One who relents concerning calamity* (Jon. 4:2).

This was God's message to the Canaanites as well as to His own people Israel as they marched over Jordan.

LESSONS FOR TODAY

There are three dynamic twentieth-century lessons that clearly emerge from this study.

First, God honors faith but He does not expect His children to operate on blind faith. Frequently Bible teachers emphasize the importance of "faith" as they teach about many of these Old Testament characters.

And, of course, it is true that faith is the focal point in many of their lives. This is very clear from Hebrews 11. But often we fail to emphasize that their faith was based squarely on facts—God's direct revelation and the promises He made to these faithful followers personally. This was true in Joshua's experience as he approached the Jordan River. He had great faith, but he also had great evidence and factual information on which to base that faith.

Today many Christians are being led astray by relying on experience and feelings which are in some instances in direct opposition to the written Word of God. Experience—even what may appear to be *Christian* experience—can lead us into some very subtle traps. We must always make sure our feelings and desires (and faith) are in harmony with Scripture. Furthermore, we must make sure the promises we claim are promises to us today. For example, God never promised you or me that He would roll back the waters of the Jordan River, nor any river, for that matter. But because He had a special purpose in mind for Joshua and the children of Israel He performed this miracle for their seeing. On the other hand God has promised us many things for our encouragement. He promised that He will never leave us nor forsake us (see Heb. 13:5; Matt. 28:20). His presence will always be with us. Our responsibility as Christians is to base our faith on the direct teachings of Scriptures that are made to all believers of all time. This means that we must read our Bible carefully and prayerfully, seeking to know His will for us today.

Another error that some Christians make is to give non-Christians the impression that Christian faith is a leap in the dark. Not so! A Christian's faith can and should be based on a reliable and trustworthy message. There is more internal and external evidence to trust the Bible and what it says than most other historical records. This statement may surprise some people, but it is factual. It is based on evidences that are well known among those who have carefully compared the history in biblical documents with the history in other literature.[1]

Second, God honors Christians who honor Him. Perhaps the most striking lesson that jumps off the pages of this Old Testament story is the way in which Joshua gave glory to God. How easy it would have been for him to honor himself when God told Joshua directly that He was going to honor him that day.

This was one of Joshua's secrets to success as an Old Testament believer. And it is one of the secrets to successful Christian living in the twentieth century. We must develop a proper balance and perspective on God's sovereign use of human beings. God does use our talents and our abilities. He actually wants us to have confidence in ourselves. He wants us to honor one another. But above all this, He wants the glory. He alone is God! He has made us! Without Him we can do nothing! Our very life and breath are in His hands.

Remember, too, that your own temptation toward pride may be accentuated because of feelings of insecurity and a lack of self-worth. This sounds strange, but it's true! Often people with this kind of problem react to success like a dry sponge responds to water. Their need for positive feedback is so great that they overreact.

Whatever the cause of persistent pride and self-glorification, it is inappropriate behavior. We need to deal with the problem, forsake pride and honor and glorify God in all we do. This does not mean that we should not accept honor and praise, but rather it means that we should develop the ability to handle them with balance and perspective. And the more we become secure within ourselves and in our Lord, the more we will be able to praise and honor God and others with naturalness and balance.

Third, God is still reaching out to lost humanity. One of God's primary purposes in calling Israel to be His special people was to use them as a nation to communicate His righteousness and love to a lost world. Today God's plan is to use His Body, the church, to communicate this truth to those who do not know Him. Thus, He prayed to His Father before returning to heaven:

> *I do not ask in behalf of these alone [His disciples], but for those also who believe in Me through their word [all Christians of all time]; that they may all be one ... I in them, and Thou in Me, that they may be perfected in unity,* **that the world may know that Thou didst send Me,** *and didst love them, even as Thou didst love Me* (John 17:20,21,23).

Peter also exhorted regarding God's purpose in reaching the world:

> *But you are a chosen race, a royal priesthood, a holy nation, a people for God's own possession, that you may proclaim the excellencies of Him who has called you out of darkness into His marvelous light; for you once were not a people, but now you are the people of God; you had not received mercy, but now you have received mercy.*
>
> *Beloved, I urge you as aliens and strangers to abstain from fleshly lusts, which wage war against the soul.*
>
> *Keep your behavior excellent among the Gentiles, so that in the thing in which they slander you as evildoers, they may on account of your good deeds, as they observe them, glorify God in the day of visitation* (1 Pet. 2:9-12).

LIFE RESPONSE

The following questions will enable you to apply these lessons to your life personally. Zero in on the question that is most appropriate to your own spiritual need and decide today what you can do to be more effective as a Christian in that area of your life.

1. To what extent am I trusting God based on a thorough knowledge of His Word and how it applies to me today?

☐ *never* ☐ *a little* ☐ *some* ☐ *much*

2. To what extent am I giving glory and honor to God for what He has given me? Conversely, to what extent do I glorify and honor myself rather than others and the God I serve?

☐ *never* ☐ *a little* ☐ *some* ☐ *much*

3. To what extent am I contributing to the effectiveness of Christ's Body, the church, in order to provide a corporate image of love, unity and righteousness to the unsaved world?

☐ *never* ☐ *a little* ☐ *some* ☐ *much*

FOLLOW-UP PROJECT

Following are some verses that relate to the practical lessons in this chapter. Memorize those that correspond to the spiritual need you are most concerned about. Type these verses on a card and put them in a location in your home or office where they will serve as a constant reminder and challenge.

> • *Since therefore, brethren, we have confidence to enter the holy place by the blood of Jesus, by a new and living way which He inaugurated for us through the veil, that is, His flesh, and since we have a great priest over the house of God, let us draw near with a sincere heart* **in full assurance of faith**, *having our hearts sprinkled clean from an evil con-*

science and our body washed with pure water. Let us hold fast the confession of our hope without wavering, for He who promised is faithful (Heb. 10:19-23).

• Whether, then, you eat or drink or whatever you do, do all to the glory of God. Give no offense either to Jews or to Greeks or to the church of God; just as I also please all men in all things, not seeking my own profit, but the profit of the many, that they may be saved (1 Cor. 10:31-33).

• I, therefore, the prisoner of the Lord, entreat you to walk in a manner worthy of the calling with which you have been called, with all humility and gentleness, with patience, showing forbearance to one another in love, being diligent **to preserve the unity of the Spirit** in the bond of peace (Eph. 4:1-3).

Note

1. For a very helpful summation of these evidences consult Josh McDowell's two volumes—*Evidence That Demands a Verdict* and *More Evidence That Demands a Verdict* (Arrowhead Springs, CA: Campus Crusade for Christ). Both of these books will increase your faith in the reliability of the Scriptures.

MEMORIAL
STONES

The Memorial Stones (Josh. 4:1-5,9-20)
The Purpose of the Memorial Stones (Josh. 4:6,7,21-24)
The Ultimate Results (Judg. 2:8-15)

I had the privilege of being reared in a Christian
family. Though my parents were quite involved in legalistic Christianity, they were different from most. There
was a reality about their lives I shall never forget. They
never forced us to accept their faith or their standards
of conduct, but they consistently loved us, provided for
us and demonstrated their trust and faith in God. And
they never hesitated to teach us what God said in the
Bible.

Though cultural values have changed drastically since
my childhood and adolescent years, I still believe in the
values I was taught as a child. True, I refined my convictions in the light of the teachings of Scripture, but my
heritage still stands. I thank God for my Christian parents.

71

Unfortunately, not everyone has the benefit of God-honoring parents. Parents today, just as parents in Joshua's day, fail to obey God in this respect.

THE MEMORIAL STONES (Josh. 4:1-5,9-20)

God taught the children of Israel many important spiritual truths on their journey from Egypt to Canaan but none was more important than the lesson surrounding the "memorial stones." Whether or not they took this lesson to heart would, in many respects, determine their future destiny as a nation.

God had just worked another great miracle for Israel. He caused the raging waters of the Jordan River to rise "up in one heap . . . while all Israel crossed on dry ground" (Josh. 3:16,17). Miraculously, when the priests, who were carrying the Ark of the Covenant, stepped into the river the rushing waters that were flowing toward the Dead Sea were suddenly cut off. Many years earlier when they had crossed the Red Sea the children of Israel were leaving the land of bondage (Egypt). As they now crossed over the Jordan they were entering a land that promised to be a place of freedom (Canaan). There was, however, a stipulation. They must meet God's conditions. And God's instructions regarding the "memorial stones" in Joshua 4 serve as another important reminder to Israel of His conditions for being able to enter the land victoriously and to enjoy the blessings He had promised.

Before the priests ever stepped foot into the Jordan River, God had given Joshua some general instructions regarding what should happen once they crossed the river. Twelve men were selected, one from each tribe, to carry out the rest of God's plan as soon as the children of Israel crossed over Jordan (see Josh. 3:12). And once they "had finished crossing" the Lord gave more specific instructions. Joshua was to command these men to go back to the center of the riverbed where the priests were still standing, holding the ark. From the "middle of the Jordan" each man was to pick up a large rock or stone and carry it to the side of the river where Israel now camped in the land of Canaan (see 4:3-5).

At this point we can imagine what may have passed through the minds of these 12 men. Go back into the middle of the Jordan? No doubt Israel had taken the better part of the day to complete the crossing. And the waters were still piled high, the ground still dry! But how long would it last? Nevertheless, the men obeyed God's instructions. Whatever fear they may have felt was not allowed to dominate and control their human desires and reactions. By faith they reentered the riverbed,

> . . . and took up twelve stones from the middle of the Jordan, just as the Lord spoke to Joshua, according to the number of the tribes of the sons of Israel; and they carried them over with them to the lodging place, and put them down there (4:8).

There may have been another reason why these men obeyed God so readily. Joshua not only issued God's order, but he personally joined these men on their rather strange mission back into the riverbed. Should the Jordan suddenly return to normal, it would have taken not only the lives of the 12 men and the priests, who still faithfully stood in the middle of the river holding the ark, but Joshua's life as well. And in view of God's promises to this man, there was little chance that this would happen. Together, these men courageously tackled this task.

But something very interesting happened once they arrived in the middle of the Jordan. While the 12 men were transporting their stones back to the shore, Joshua, in his excitement, suddenly began to pile up stones in the middle of the river, right at the feet of the priests. There is no record that God had instructed him to do this. Probably it was a spontaneous act of worship. Joshua already knew what God's purpose was in having them carry the stones *from* Jordan, so he simply decided to pile up 12 stones *in* Jordan as a personal testimony to what God had done for Israel in backing up the waters of the Jordan River. The text tells us that these stones "are there to this day" (4:9).

This statement does not mean of course that these 12 stones are still stacked up in the middle of the Jordan River to *our* present day. Rather, it means that at the time of the writing of the historical record and the book of Joshua, these stones still stood as a tribute to God's great power. Perhaps when the waters subsided to a normal level they became even more visible. And as the waters rose and fell over the next several years, each time the stones stood out as a memorial to God's love and care for Israel. But why did they take the stones from the middle of the Jordan to the lodging place?

THE PURPOSE OF THE MEMORIAL STONES
(Josh. 4:6,7,21-24)

When the 12 men completed their task of carrying the 12 stones to the shore of Canaan, and after Joshua built an altar in the middle of the river with 12 more stones, Joshua then commanded the priests to proceed across the river with the Ark of the Covenant. The moment their feet touched the other side, the wall of water that had piled up for miles back up the river came crashing downward. We read, "The waters of the Jordan returned to their place, and went over all its banks as before" (4:18).

What an awe-inspiring sight this must have been for the children of Israel as they stood in the land of Canaan watching the completion of this great miracle. But following their shouts of joy and triumph there must have been a gradual silence that crept over them. Everything seemed so normal again. The water was rushing and swirling down to the Dead Sea as it had before. For some the whole experience may have been like a dream. Did this really happen? That very morning they had stood on the one side of the mighty rushing Jordan. Now they were on the other side. How could it be?

But it was true. The children of Israel moved on to Gilgal (see map 3, p. 57) carrying the 12 stones from the Jordan, proof that the experience was no dream. It was a reality. And there in Gilgal the stones were set up as a memorial (see 4:20).

God stated the purpose for these stones at the same time He instructed Joshua to have the 12 men from each tribe transport them from the middle of the river. And Joshua shared this purpose with these men prior to their involvement in the project (see 4:6,7). But the most complete statement of purpose is found at the end of this chapter when Joshua spoke to all the people of Israel as the stones were being set up in Gilgal.

The purpose was two-fold: First, these stones were to remind Israel and succeeding generations that God is a God of great power and glory and it was He who brought them over Jordan. Thus, Joshua said to the sons of Israel:

> *When your children ask their fathers in time to come, saying, 'What are these stones?' then you shall inform your children, saying, 'Israel crossed this Jordan on dry ground.' For the Lord your God dried up the waters of the Jordan before you until you had crossed, just as the Lord your God had done to the Red Sea, which He dried up before us until we had crossed* (4:21-23).

The purpose of these stones was not only to remind

Israel of what God had done, but "*that all the peoples of the earth* may know that the hand of the Lord is mighty, so that you may fear the Lord your God forever*" (4:24).

Once again we see God's great concern for all mankind. One of His primary purposes in choosing Israel and loving them as His own chosen people was to use them as a dramatic means to communicate to lost humanity that He is a God who cares about their eternal destiny. And the message was heard! It went throughout the whole land! We read:

> *Now it came about when all the kings of the Amorites who were beyond the Jordan to the west, and all the kings of the Canaanites who were by the sea, heard how the Lord had dried up the waters of the Jordan before the sons of Israel until they had crossed, that their hearts melted, and there was no spirit in them any longer, because of the sons of Israel* (5:1).

THE ULTIMATE RESULTS (Judg. 2:8-15)

How wonderful it would be if we could report that the Canaanites, upon seeing and hearing about this great demonstration of God's power and loving concern for Israel, repented of their sins, turned from their wicked ways and joined Israel in following the one true God. But they didn't! Like Pharaoh in Egypt, who actually experienced the great plagues, their fears soon turned to pride and arrogance. They hardened their hearts against God and refused to acknowledge who He really is!

How tragic! But even more tragic, God's own chosen people, Israel, failed to remind their children of what God had done. No sooner had they settled into the land flowing with milk and honey than their memories began to fade. Even the memorial stones were forgotten by the majority in Israel.

One of the most heartbreaking historical statements in all of the Bible is recorded in Judges 2. Many years had passed since Israel crossed over Jordan and set up the memorial stones in Gilgal and God had given them victory after victory. After years of bondage and wilderness wanderings they settled into the land and enjoyed the freedom of having a place to live in peace and plenty. But something was happening to Israel. The end result is almost unbelievable. We read:

> Then Joshua the son of Nun, the servant of the Lord, died at the age of one hundred and ten .... and all that generation also were gathered to their fathers; and there arose another generation after them who did not know the Lord, nor yet the work which He had done for Israel (Judg. 2:8,10).

How could this be? How could a people who had witnessed the miracles of God ever forget them? Nevertheless, the parents in Israel failed to tell their children what God had done for them at Jordan and how He continued to give them victories over their enemies. Consequently, their children turned away from God and "did evil" and "served the Baals" in Canaan.

> They forsook the Lord, the God of their fathers, who had brought them out of the land of Egypt, and followed other gods from among the gods of the peoples who were around them, and bowed themselves down to them; thus they provoked the Lord to anger (Judg. 2:12).

In two generations all of Israel had forsaken the God who was responsible for everything they had.

LESSONS FOR TODAY

It is difficult for many of us living today to comprehend how such a thing could happen in such a short period of time. But think for a moment about what has happened in the American culture in the last 30 years: our whole value system has changed and this change has affected the family. When parents cease to reflect God's values in their home, it only takes *one generation* for spiritual *degeneration* to take place. When we as parents fail to teach our children, by word and example, respect and love for God and His Word, when we fail to communicate to them who He is—we are on the road to spiritual disaster. In America this has become a reciprocal interacting process. As society has changed, so has the family. And as the family has changed, it has increased the changes in society.

If we go back to the beginning of our American culture, it is easy to detect that our society reflected a biblical value system in our marital and family life, in our business ethics, in our recreational and entertainment activities, in our academic institutions and in government. Don't misunderstand! I am not suggesting we were ever a Christian nation. Rather, we were a nation built upon the value system that grew out of the Hebrew-Christian ethic as we saw it spelled out in the Bible. Though many people, including our early presidents, did not profess a personal faith in Jesus Christ as the Son of God, many of them nevertheless wrote into the laws of the land a system of values that reflected the teachings of Scripture.

Over the years our value system as a nation has changed dramatically, particularly in the last 20 to 30 years. In some respects there is very little overlap between what the Bible says is right and wrong and what our culture accepts as right and wrong. In many cases we still verbalize the old values but in reality we do not abide by them in our daily activities. We have moved from believing in a system of absolutes to a completely relativistic approach in making decisions in the area of personal and social ethics (see diagram 1).

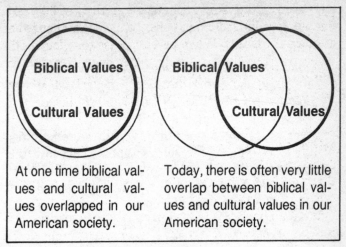

At one time biblical values and cultural values overlapped in our American society.

Today, there is often very little overlap between biblical values and cultural values in our American society.

Diagram 1

Unfortunately many American families (even Christian families) are being seriously influenced and affected by our changing value system. They are finding it difficult to be in the world without being a part of the world (see John 17:14-16). The fact is, our thinking has, in many instances, become confused and out of focus. The impact of the media (television, movies, literature), and particularly of our educational institutions, has little by little influenced our thinking in ways we are not even aware of.

This was Israel's problem in Canaan. God warned them very early in their journey from Egypt to Canaan not to allow the environment they were going into to cause them to fail to acknowledge Him and to teach their children who He was and what He had done for them. God said through Moses:

Watch yourself, lest you forget the Lord who brought you from the land of Egypt, out of the house of slavery. You shall fear only the Lord your God; and you shall worship Him,

79

*and swear by His name. You shall not follow
other gods, any of the gods of the peoples who
surround you, for the Lord your God in the
midst of you is a jealous God; otherwise the
anger of the Lord your God will be kindled
against you, and He will wipe you off the face
of the earth* (Deut. 6:12-15).

Later Moses made the warning even more specific,
spelling out some of the things that could cause the
Israelites to forget the Lord.

*For the Lord your God is bringing you into
a good land, a land of brooks of water, of
fountains and springs, flowing forth in valleys
and hills; a land of wheat and barley, of vines
and fig trees and pomegranates, a land of olive
oil and honey; a land where you shall eat food
without scarcity, in which you shall not lack
anything; a land whose stones are iron, and
out of whose hills you can dig copper. When
you have eaten and are satisfied, you shall
bless the Lord your God for the good land
which He has given you. Beware lest you forget the Lord your God by not keeping His
commandments and His ordinances and His
statutes which I am commanding you today;
lest, when you have eaten and are satisfied,
and have built good houses and lived in them,
and when your herds and your flocks multiply, and your silver and gold multiply, and all
that you have multiplies* **then your heart
becomes proud, and you forget the Lord your
God** *who brought you out from the land of
Egypt, out of the house of slavery* (Deut. 8:7-
14).

Unfortunately, Israel forgot these warnings. And
when the new generation that was eventually allowed to

enter Canaan was reminded of these truths with the memorial stones, they even forgot to use these stones as God intended. They failed to teach their children about the one who brought them over Jordan. So one generation later they were involved in unbelievable materialism, idolatry and immorality. Consequently, God's hand of judgment fell on them and they were eventually scattered to the ends of the earth.

What is happening in your home and mine? What will our children remember about us? Will they remember a beautiful home, color television, the latest model automobile, a lake lot, a boat, an open-ended allowance—and all the frantic efforts we put forth to accumulate these possessions?

God does not say that material things are wrong. If they are wrong why would He have given the children of Israel all the things mentioned in Deuteronomy 6 and 8? Both Abraham and Job would be millionaries by today's standards (see Job 42:10-12).

Material things, therefore, are not the issue. Our attitude toward the God of heaven is! The children of Israel became materialists. They took the credit for the blessings they had received from God. Eventually they turned away from God to false gods—the gods of a pagan society. And, in the process, they failed to teach consistently their children their sacred history.

What about us? Do we even have any memorial stones that can remind us and our children about God's blessings?

LIFE RESPONSE

Answer the following questions as honestly as possible. Write out one thing you can do immediately to help your children sense the reality of God. (As a single person you might think of one thing you can do to help your Christian friends know the reality of God.) Pray and ask God to help you reach your objective.

1. What evidences are there in my home, in my personal life, that God exists and that we are dependent upon Him for life and existence?

2. In what ways do we talk about God? As a living reality? As a household fetish? Someone we talk about because we are supposed to?

3. In what ways can I convey to my children a reverence and respect for God? In what ways can I convey to my children that everything we have comes from Him? What memorial stones are there in my home and family life that are constant reminders of the greatness and power of God?

FOLLOW-UP PROJECT

Memorize Matthew 6:33:

> *But seek first His kingdom, and His righteousness; and all these things shall be added to you.*

MORE REMEMBRANCES

The Rite of Circumcision (Josh. 5:2-9)
The Passover (Josh. 5:10-12)
Holy Ground (Josh. 5:13-15)

Though my early church background left much to be desired when measured by biblical standards, there are some things I will never forget. The church ordinances, such as baptism and communion—those things we do "in remembrance" of what God has done for us—were special. I'll never forget my own baptismal service. The death and resurrection of Christ became very real to me. Though I was quite confused in other doctrinal areas in my Christian life, I understood the true meaning of the ordinances.

Today these ordinances are even more meaningful to me. One thing I've learned rather recently from the study of the New Testament is that they are not only for Christians to practice but for non-Christians to see. Properly performed in the presence of unbelievers, church ordinances can become a dynamic means for communicating the gospel of Jesus Christ.

This chapter introduces you to some Old Testament ordinances that in many respects set the stage for the New Testament ones. In Israel they were not only remembrances, they were also a witness to the pagan people surrounding them.

God knows how easily people forget! This is why He instructed Joshua to remove 12 stones from the middle of the Jordan River and to stack them up at Gilgal. They were to be a memorial to God's great power in bringing the nation of Israel into the Promised Land. They were to be a means of communicating to their children that indeed God had "dried up the waters of the Jordan" just as He "had done to the Red Sea." The purpose was to demonstrate before "all the peoples of the earth . . . that the hand of the Lord is mighty" and that Israel and all mankind "may fear the Lord" (Josh. 4:23,24).

Giving Israel symbols to help them remember His acts of love and grace was not a new phenomenon. And as we'll see later, God continued to provide remembrances for His children even in New Testament days. Our memories *are* short. And God has taken that into consideration in His great plan for mankind.

THE RITE OF CIRCUMCISION (Josh. 5:2-9)

Once this new generation of Israelites had entered the land of Canaan, the Lord instructed Joshua to make sure *all* the sons of Israel were circumcised (5:2). God's reasoning behind this command is stated clearly:

> *And this is the reason why Joshua circumcised them: all the people who came out of Egypt who were males, all the men of war, died in the wilderness along the way, after they came out of Egypt. For all the people who came out were circumcised, but all the people*

who were born in the wilderness along the way
as they came out of Egypt had not been cir-
cumcised (5:4,5)

Circumcision was a rite established by God when He
first called Abraham out of paganism and covenanted
with him that He would bless Abraham with a *land*, a
seed, and a *blessing* (see Gen. 12:1-3). The "land" was
Canaan! The "seed" was the nation Israel! And the
"blessing" was the Saviour who would come into the
world to die for the sins of all mankind!

God confirmed that covenant with Abraham by
means of circumcision. It was a "sign of the covenant"
(Gen. 17:9-14). And it was to be a continual practice in
Israel to remind them of God's promises. "Every male
among you," the Lord said to Abraham, "who is eight
days old shall be circumcised *throughout your genera-*
tions" (Gen. 17:12).

Why did God choose circumcision as a sign of His
covenant? First, we must realize that God's ways are
often not our ways. He does things at times that are
difficult for our finite minds to grasp. Where our reasoning ends, His begins (see Isa. 55:8,9; Rom. 11:33). On
the other hand, most of the things that God does and the
demands He makes of His people make sense, particularly if we stop for a moment and think about it histori-
cally, culturally and scientifically. Whenever God acts
He usually achieves more than one purpose with the
same event or situation.

This is definitely true of circumcision. Let's begin
with a secondary purpose. About 4,000 years after
God's command to Abraham regarding circumcision,
medical science discovered that wives of men who had
not been circumcised have a larger incidence of cancer
of the cervix than do wives of men who have been
circumcised. This is particularly true in primitive cultures where personal cleanliness is an environmental

problem. Putting it plain and simple, circumcision promotes personal hygiene and helps eliminate virulent bacteria including the "cancer-producing Smegma bacillus."[1]

God was not only selecting a means that had spiritual significance but healthful benefits. Part of God's promise to Abraham was a *seed*—multitudes of children and grandchildren for generations to come. And with that promise of multiplication God selected the rite of circumcision as a personal protection from one of the most serious causes of death—cancer. And of even greater significance, even with all of our scientific knowledge, we have not to this day discovered a satisfactory cure for this deadly disease.

One other interesting sidelight is the fact that God commanded the parents of Israel to circumcise their male children on the *eighth day* following their birth (see Gen. 17:12). Again, medical science has discovered that this is the best time in a child's life to perform this minor operation. Natural resources in the human body for preventing excessive bleeding reach a 110 percent level about the eighth day and then level off quickly following this point in time. Furthermore, before the eighth day, these natural resources have not yet been produced in sufficient quantity in the child's body to make the operation generally safe.[2] Once again we see God's wisdom in prescribing this specific rite as a sign of His covenant with Israel.

Scientific explanations for this symbolic act, however, are only secondary purposes. God's primary reasons for circumcision were spiritual.

First, no male child in Israel could miss this constant reminder that he was different from other male children who were not Israelites. There were many natural opportunities in these primitive cultures for parents to explain to both the male and female children *why* little boys were circumcised. Circumcision served as a constant reminder to Israel and the pagans around them of God's covenant with His chosen people.

Second, no adult male would ever be able to forget God's covenant. Several times a day he would be reminded as he performed natural body functions.

Third, no wife in Israel would be able to forget. With every intimate relationship with her husband she was reminded that God had made a promise to them.

Fourth, no man in Israel would ever be able to engage in illicit sexual activities with a pagan woman without being confronted with the fact that he was different from other males—a definite reminder of his chosen position in God's eternal plan. Even an act of sin would bring to his remembrance God's covenant.

Stating it very clearly, when measured by scientific, cultural, historical and spiritual criteria, there is no organ in the human body that could be chosen by God to achieve His divine purposes more adequately than the male sexual organ. And this ought also to say something to us about God's view of natural processes—from elimination to legitimate sexual relationships. Mankind perverts and makes unclean what God has created to be very natural and necessary. In fact, it is so natural and meaningful to God, that He chose circumcision as a spiritual reminder of His own *personal relationship* with His people.

When the children of Israel entered Canaan after crossing the Jordan, God once again reminded them of His covenant. And to help them remember that covenant, He instructed them to once again circumcise all the males in Israel. With this act God also removed the "reproach of Egypt" from them (Josh. 5:9). The Egyptians had scoffed at the Israelites, suggesting that God had delivered them from their land in order to "kill them in the mountains" (Exod. 32:12). On this day,

"When they had finished circumcising all the nation," they were delivered from that accusation. "Today," the Lord said to Joshua, "I have rolled away the reproach of Egypt from you" (Josh. 5:9). They were indeed God's chosen people and He would never renege on His promise to Abraham. It was *unconditional, literal* and *eternal*.

THE PASSOVER (Josh. 5:10-12)

While the children of Israel were still in Egyptian bondage God instituted another remembrance of His love and grace. It was the Passover, a special event connected with Israel's deliverance from slavery. After sending nine plagues on Egypt, God revealed that He was going to bring one final catastrophe on them—He was going to slay all the firstborn, "from the first-born of the Pharaoh who sits on his throne, even to the first-born of the slave girl who is behind the millstones; all the first-born of the cattle as well" (Exod. 11:5). However, the children of Israel would be spared from this judgment if they sprinkled the blood of a lamb or goat on the doorposts of their houses. "When I see the blood," the Lord promised, "I will pass over you, and no plague will befall you to destroy you when I strike the land of Egypt" (Exod. 12:13).

And so it happened just as God said it would. Judgment fell. And all the families in Israel who had prepared themselves according to God's instructions were spared. It was very clear that God intended for Israel to remember the Lord's mercy perpetually by practicing the Passover. We read:

> *Now this day will be a memorial to you, and you shall celebrate it as a feast to the Lord; throughout your generations you are to celebrate it as a permanent ordinance* (Exod. 12: 14).

Consequently, serious-minded Jews, even to this day, remember their deliverance from Egypt by engaging in the Passover and the Feast of Unleavened Bread.[3]

As far as we can tell from the scriptural record, the Passover was kept only twice preceding the events recorded in Joshua 5. The first time was on the evening before the Israelites left Egypt. The second time was in the wilderness of Sinai, a year after they left the land of bondage (see Num. 9:1-5). And the third time was *now* —after the children of Israel wandered in the wilderness for 40 years and as a new generation entered Canaan. The celebration followed their experience in setting up the memorial stones and after reinstating the rite of circumcision.

It is very clear what God had in mind. He was concerned that the children of Israel never forget all the things He had done for them. The *memorial stones* would remind them and their children of His great power in parting the waters of the Red Sea and backing up the Jordan River. *Circumcision* would help them to remember His unconditional covenant which He first gave to Abraham. And the *Passover* would remind them of His love and grace in sparing them from the horrible plague in Egypt.

To add to the drama of this occasion, following the Passover meal the manna that God had provided regularly—even when they were being judged for their sins as they wandered in the wilderness—ceased. For the first time, the children of Israel were able to eat "some of the yield of the land of Canaan," a direct fulfillment of God's promise to them many years before (see Exod. 13:35; Josh. 5:12).

HOLY GROUND (Josh. 5:13-15)

The grand culmination for all of these events involved a very personal experience for Joshua, very reminiscent of Moses' experience when God spoke to him from a burning bush as he was "pasturing the flock of Jethro his father-in-law" (Exod. 3:1). There on the west side of the desert an angel of the Lord called to him out of the middle of the bush and told him to remove his sandals from his feet, for, said the angel, "the place on which you are standing is holy ground" (Exod. 3:5).

Joshua's experience following the Passover was similar to Moses' burning bush encounter. While he was preparing to attack Jericho, an armed man with a sword suddenly appeared to him. He identified himself as "captain of the host of the Lord." Joshua immediately recognized God's presence in this man and he "fell on his face" and worshiped Him (Josh. 5:13,14).

Unlike Moses, it was not necessary for God to get Joshua's attention. He was already involved in his role as leader of Israel. The most significant similarity is that God was revealing to Joshua that the ground where he was standing at that moment was indeed holy because of God's awesome presence as He spoke to His servant by means of an angel. Furthermore, God was no doubt communicating to Joshua that the *entire land*—the land of Canaan—was also holy; that is, it was set apart for them and some day they would have it as their very own. God's will, of course, was that His people Israel would use that land as a means to reflect His holiness to all the peoples of the earth. Their lives were to reflect God's righteousness.

LESSONS FOR TODAY

The most obvious application to our lives today as twentieth-century Christians is that we too, like the children of Israel, have short memories. We too need remembrances lest we forget what God has done for us. And just as God instituted memorial events in the Old Testament, so He instituted some very unique memorial events in the New Testament, which, as Christians, we are to practice to this day.

The first of these is baptism. In the first century when people were converted to Jesus Christ, they were baptized. And this was a fulfillment of the Lord's will, for He instructed His followers to "go therefore and make disciples of all the nations, *baptizing them* in the name of the Father and the Son and the Holy Spirit" (Matt. 28:19). And this they did!

Baptism, like circumcision in the Old Testament, is a sign. It is not a means of salvation, as some people teach, but rather, is a symbolic representation of Christ's death and resurrection. Personally I believe that the Bible teaches it should be for believers only—people who are old enough to make an intelligent decision for Jesus Christ. The best form for baptism, it seems, is immersion, though some well-respected Christian scholars disagree on the mode. The important thing is clear, however. Baptism is to remind us and the world that Jesus died and rose again and that by faith in Him we are buried with Him and raised to a new life. Every Christian who wants to be completely obedient to Christ should be baptized.

The second memorial event is communion. When Jesus was eating the Passover supper with the apostles just before His death on the cross, He extended the significance of this religious meal into the life of the Body of Christ, the church. As He broke the bread that evening with His followers and drank the cup with them, He demonstrated how His body would be given and His blood shed for the sins of the world. "Do this," He said, "in remembrance of Me" (Luke 22:19). And Paul built on Christ's words in his letter to the Corinthians when he wrote, "For as often as you eat this bread and drink the cup, you proclaim the Lord's death until He comes" (1 Cor. 11:26).

Down through church history Christians have remembered the Lord with this ordinance. It has taken many forms—from a full meal to a token meal. The form, it seems, is not really that important. But the meaning is! The communion is a remembrance—a remembrance of Christ's death for each of us and for the sins of the world. Like Israel, we need a constant reminder that when God sees the blood—in this instance the blood of Christ—He will pass over us in judgment. By the blood of the perfect Lamb of God, His Son Jesus Christ, we have been cleansed from our sins and set free from eternal judgment and death. "In Him [Christ] we have redemption through His blood, the forgiveness of our trespasses, according to the riches of His grace" (Eph. 1:7).

Circumcision of the heart is a third remembrance. Even in Old Testament days these external signs were a means to help people experience internal realities. This is why Paul wrote that "they are not all Israel who are descended from Israel" (Rom. 9:6). Furthermore, wrote Paul,

> *For he is not a Jew who is one outwardly; neither is circumcision that which is outward in the flesh; but he is a Jew who is one inwardly; and circumcision is that which is of the heart, by the Spirit, not by the letter; and his praise is not from men, but from God* (Rom. 2:28,29).

Circumcision is no longer necessary as an ordinance from God. Though it is certainly medically recommended, it has no spiritual significance since Christ came to fulfill the demands of God's law. In Christ we "have been made complete." In Christ we have been "circumcised with a circumcision made without hands" (Col. 2:10,11). And today we are to reveal His grace through our *total being*—body, soul and spirit (see

Rom. 12:1,2). We are His children, and people everywhere should know that we are different, not because of the "circumcision of our flesh" but because of the "circumcision of our hearts." Indeed, we too are standing on holy ground—daily! Through Christ we can enter into the very presence of God. With confidence we can "enter the holy place by the blood of Jesus, by a new and living way which He inaugurated for us through the veil, that is, *His flesh*" (Heb. 10:19,20). We need not fear. We need not remove our shoes or maintain a particular posture. But always we should "draw near with a sincere heart in full assurance of faith" (Heb. 10:22) and always we should reflect His character and His love so that all men will know that we are children of God.

LIFE RESPONSE

Consider the following questions:

1. Have I been baptized since I became a Christian?

2. Am I a part of a group where I regularly remember the Lord through holy communion?

NOTE: God does not specify when or where or how often we should take communion. It is to be regular and meaningful, preceded by self-examination (see 1 Cor. 11:28). And neither does the Bible specify who should serve communion. For example, Christian fathers have the privilege of having communion with their families. Indeed, this is a beautiful experience in family worship and teaching and probably was normative in the New Testament world, since many New Testament churches were house churches, many beginning with one family unit.

3. Am I truly converted to Jesus Christ, having been circumcised in heart through the operation of the Holy Spirit? Furthermore, as a Christian, am I reflecting Christ's righteousness and love to all men, revealing that I am indeed a new person in Christ?

FOLLOW-UP PROJECT

Meditate on Colossians 2:9-14:

> *For in Him all the fulness of Deity dwells in bodily form, and in Him you have been made complete, and He is the head over all rule and authority; and in Him you were also circumcised with a circumcision made without hands, in the removal of the body of the flesh by the circumcision of Christ; having been buried with Him in baptism, in which you were also raised up with Him through faith in the working of God, who raised Him from the dead. And when you were dead in your transgressions and the uncircumcision of your flesh, He made you alive together with Him, having forgiven us all our transgressions, having cancelled out the certificate of debt consisting of decrees against us and which was hostile to us; and He has taken it out of the way, having nailed it to the cross.*

Notes

1. For research data see S.I. McMillen, *None of These Diseases* (Old Tappan, New Jersey: Fleming H. Revell Company, 1963), pp. 17-22.
2. Ibid, pp. 20,21.
3. The Passover is designated as the *sacrifice* and the feast following the sacrifice is designated as the Feast of Unleavened Bread. These two events are inseparably related and are often simply called "the Passover."

VICTORY AT JERICHO

The Lord's Command (Josh. 6:2-5)
The People Obey (Josh. 6:6-19)
Jericho Is Captured (Josh. 6:20-27)
God's Missionary Methodology (1 Kings 8:41-43)

One thing that used to be very difficult for me to understand and accept was God's judgment on pagan people in the Old Testament. Today I have a much different perspective.

Take for example God's judgment on Jericho. Some people conclude (I did at one time) that the Lord suddenly decided to wipe those people off the face of the earth. Not so! Rahab tells us that they had known about the God of Israel for at least 40 years. They had heard of all He had done to the Egyptians because of their sins. They knew what had happened to those who opposed Israel in the wilderness. They knew about the miracle at Jordan. Furthermore, the Lord gave the people of Jericho seven days to turn from their sins as Israel marched around the city. Putting it more specifically, God never judged people (including Sodom and Gomorrah) without warning them time and time again that He was going to judge them because of their idolatry and immorality. Again and again we see God's missionary methodology in the Old Testament as He demonstrated His love and grace through Israel. It is true that few people repented, but when they did God relented and preserved them.

It is not God's desire to judge people. His attitude toward mankind has *always* been the same as that expressed by the apostle Peter: "Not wishing for any to perish but for all to come to repentance" (2 Pet. 3:9).

The children of Israel were now in the land of Canaan —a dream come true! They'd crossed the river and once again were reminded of God's great power (through the miracle at Jordan), His unconditional covenant with them (through the rite of circumcision), and His grace in delivering them from Egyptian bondage (through the Passover). They were now ready to take the land through military confrontations. The city of Jericho was, by God's direct command, to be their first target.

The people in Jericho were terribly frightened, according to the message Rahab conveyed to Israel (see Josh. 2:10,11). Not only had they heard about the Red Sea fiasco for the pursuing Egyptians some 40 years earlier, but more recently they had received reports of how the two kings of the Amorites beyond Jordan, along with all their people had been literally wiped off the face of the earth (see Num. 21:33-35). And when God rolled back the waters of the rushing and swirling Jordan River so Israel could cross on dry ground, "their hearts melted, and there was no spirit in them any longer" (Josh. 5:1). Thus we read that "Jericho was tightly shut because of the sons of Israel" and "no one went out and no one came in" (6:1). They were taking no chances. Somehow they believed they could protect themselves from the God of Israel by man-made walls—not facing the fact that those walls of brick were just as much subject to God's power as the waters of the Red Sea and of the Jordan. If God can control and manipulate natural phenomena, how much more can He conquer man-made structures. Foolish? Yes! But how common for men and women who do not know God and who are blinded by their self-centered life-styles and pagan religions to believe that they can wall out God.

THE LORD'S COMMAND (Josh. 6:2-5)

Attacking Jericho was God's will and command to Israel. This was no human idea or endeavor. The Lord's instructions were very specific, down to the last detail.

God prepared Joshua in a special way for this battle. As we've already seen, the process began in the previous chapter. "The captain of the Lord's host," who was probably God Himself in human form, appeared to Joshua while he was surveying Jericho. Revealing Himself as a man prepared for battle, the Lord instructed Joshua to remove his sandals from his feet for the place where he was standing was holy ground (see Josh. 5:13-15).[1]

Joshua's initial preparation for the battle that lay ahead was spiritual. And indeed this was important, for it would be no ordinary battle. What God was about to command Joshua to do was strange indeed compared to ordinary battle techniques. All of Israel needed to be prepared spiritually and emotionally to obey what would appear to be ridiculous and bizarre battle instructions.

But Joshua's heart *was* prepared! His response was immediate. How could he doubt now? Had God not proved faithful in the face of impossible situations? If the Lord could roll back the waters of Jordan, it would be no problem for Him to get the Israelites inside the walls of Jericho.

Actually, verses 2-5 in chapter 6 are a continuation of God's revelation in verses 13-15 in chapter 5. Once the Lord had prepared Joshua spiritually, He gave him specific instructions for attacking Jericho:

> *See, I have given Jericho into your hand, with its king and the valiant warriors. And you shall march around the city, all the men of war circling the city once. You shall do so for six days. Also seven priests shall carry seven trumpets of rams' horns before the ark; then on the seventh day you shall march around the city seven times, and the priests shall blow the trumpets. And it shall be that when they make a long blast with the ram's horn, and when you hear the sound of the trumpet, all the people shall shout with a great shout; and the wall of the city will fall down flat, and the people will go up every man straight ahead* (Josh. 6:2-5).

What we have in these short verses is a succinct statement from the Lord summarizing the remainder of chapter 6. What follows is God's instructions, worked out in the lives of the children of Israel. Joshua and the people obeyed God's orders. Consequently, they captured the city just as the Lord said they would.

THE PEOPLE OBEY (Josh. 6:6-19)

Imagine what must have been going through the minds of the inhabitants of Jericho as they watched the children of Israel from inside their fortressed walls. What a strange sight indeed! Soldiers were marching around the city. In the middle of the procession, priests of God carried the Ark of the Covenant and still others blew rams' horns. But, just as God commanded, none of the Israelites said a word.

The same thing happened the second day and the

third—until six days elapsed. And then came the seventh day. But this was different. As before, they began the procession early in the morning, but the soldiers of Israel didn't return to camp after encircling the walls the first time. They marched around a second time and a third—until they had marched around seven complete times. By now there must have been utter consternation inside the walls. What was going on? What was this unbelievable demonstration?

Then it happened: For the first time in a week, the Israelites' voices rang out. At the sound of the trumpet they shouted a "great shout" and the walls of Jericho came crashing to the ground (6:20).

What kind of walls surrounded Jericho? John Garstang, a noted archaeologist, discovered what he believed were the very walls of Jericho that fell down. He observed that there were two walls—an outer one 6 feet thick and an inner one 12 feet thick—separated by a 15-foot space. Later data, however, indicate that Garstang had assigned the wrong walls to Joshua's day and that Jericho's walls were made of mud brick and probably have eroded away over the years, leaving no archaeological evidence.

Why did the walls come tumbling down with so little effort? Some scholars believe that the walls could have collapsed because of an earthquake, since such natural phenomena are prevalent in this geographical region. Perhaps this is true, for it would be no problem for God to supernaturally synchronize an earthquake with the shout that went up from Israel's army. Either way, however—natural earthquake, supernatural earthquake, or no earthquake at all—it would still be a miracle wrought by God.[2]

JERICHO IS CAPTURED (Josh. 6:20-27)

When the walls collapsed, the army of Israel entered

Jericho and began to destroy their enemies. Caught off guard by Israel's strange strategy, the people in the city were confused and had no time to prepare to avoid the catastrophe.

God was on Israel's side. It was a supernatural victory. God had said, "I have given Jericho into your hand" (6:2). The death blow that fell on all the inhabitants of Jericho was a judgment from God because of their sin and their unrepentant hearts. Even though the Israelite army destroyed the city, the victory was God's. Israel was merely the vessel He used to accomplish His purpose.

Rahab and those members of her family who responded to her warning of coming judgment were spared. Just as the spies instructed, she had gathered her relatives into her house and hung the scarlet rope in the window. Consequently, when Israel entered Jericho,

> ... the young men who were spies went in and brought out Rahab and her father and her mother and her brothers and all she had; they also brought out all her relatives, and placed them outside the camp of Israel. And they burned the city with fire, and all that was in it .... However, Rahab the harlot and her father's household and all she had, Joshua spared; and she has lived in the midst of Israel to this day, for she hid the messengers whom Joshua sent to spy out Jericho (6:23-25).

GOD'S MISSIONARY METHODOLOGY
(1 Kings 8:41-43)

There are various interpretations in attempting to explain God's war strategy against the people of Jericho. Why would He have Israel march around Jericho for seven days? Some believe the process was solely for Israel—to teach them faith and obedience. Certainly this is involved. It did take faith for these men to obey God's instructions instead of following their natural tendency to engage in ordinary tactics of warfare.

But there seems to be another important reason, one that relates to God's missionary strategy in the Old Testament. God chose Israel in the first place, not to show favoritism or partiality, nor to demonstrate a national and narrow concern for mankind. Rather, He chose Israel to be His *means* to convey to *all nations* His existence, His sovereignty and His righteousness. He chose Israel to bear the message that He was willing to save all those, Jew or Gentile, who would truly call upon Him. Israel was to become God's unique and dramatic visual aid to convey to all men that He is a loving and merciful God, ready to save them from their sins, even though, as Paul reminded the Romans, they did not see fit to acknowledge Him (see Rom. 1:28).

Many years later when Solomon prayed to dedicate the Temple, he summarized this purpose very clearly:

> *Also concerning the foreigner who is not of Thy people Israel, when he comes from a far country for Thy name's sake (for they will hear of Thy great name and Thy mighty hand, and of Thine outstretched arm); when he comes and prays toward this house, hear Thou in heaven Thy dwelling place, and do according to all for which the foreigner calls to Thee, in order that all the peoples of the earth may know Thy name, to fear Thee, as do Thy people Israel* (1 Kings 8:41-43).

God was giving the Canaanites of Jericho one more chance to turn from their sins and their wicked ways. They had already heard of God's power in preserving Israel at the Red Sea. They had received a full description of what the Lord had done to the kings of the Amorites on the other side of Jordan. They had observed the miraculous crossing of the Jordan River. And from previous textual evidence, there's no doubt that they had descriptive reports regarding the rather major event at Gilgal—the rite of circumcision. And it is significant that this rite was a reminder to everyone that God's covenant with Israel involved giving them the land.

Furthermore, the people of Jericho probably had heard of the great plague in Egypt when all of the firstborn were slain because of Pharaoh's hardened heart. And again it is significant that the children of Israel, after they crossed the Jordan, observed the Passover reminding everyone of that great judgment God had brought on the Egyptians because of their sin and disobedience.

As Israel marched around the walls of Jericho, it seems that God is once for all saying, "Judgment is coming. Repent and turn from your sins." With each day, the final hour was growing closer. And it reached the grand crescendo on the seventh day as the people marched around the city seven times.

There are numerous events in the Old Testament to indicate that if the people in Jericho had flung open the gates and begged for mercy, turning to God and asking for forgiveness, the Lord would have relented. When Jonah warned the people of Nineveh that in "yet forty days" God would pronounce judgment on them, the people repented and God relented (Jon. 3:4-10). God would have spared Sodom and Gomorrah. In fact, God promised Abraham He would spare both cities if there were only 10 righteous people living there. God's reticence to bring judgment on Sodom and Gomorrah is clearly seen in His willingness to relent when Abraham asked Him to spare the cities if 50 righteous people could be found; then Abraham moved the number down to 45, to 40, to 30, to 20 and finally to 10. Even then

God promised He would not destroy them if Abraham could find just 10 righteous people (see Gen. 18:23-32). Of course, there were not even 10. And God's judgment fell on Sodom and Gomorrah, just as it did on Jericho.

Note too that God's judgment on Jericho was just one additional warning to the other Canaanite cities. Their turn was next. Israel was on the march—at the command of God. And with each death blow God was saying, "Repent! Repent! Repent! Turn from your wicked ways, your immoralities, your false gods, your child sacrifices and your other numerous evil deeds. And if you do, I'll preserve you as I did Rahab the harlot and her whole family."

LESSONS FOR TODAY

Even in New Testament days, just a few short years after Christ walked on this earth, there were mockers who said regarding Christ's promise to come again,

"Where is the promise of His coming? For ever since the fathers fell asleep, all continues just as it was from the beginning of creation." For when they maintain this, it escapes their notice that by the word of God the heavens existed long ago and the earth was formed out of water and by water, through which the world at that time was destroyed, being flooded with water. But the present heavens and earth by His word are being reserved for fire, kept for the day of judgment and destruction of ungodly men. But do not let this one fact escape your notice, beloved, that with the Lord one day is as a thousand years, and a thousand years as one day. The Lord is not slow about His promise, as some count slowness, but is patient toward you, not wishing for any to perish but for all to come to repentance. But

*the day of the Lord will come like a thief, in
which the heavens will pass away with a roar
and the elements will be destroyed with intense
heat, and the earth and its works will be
burned up* (2 Pet. 3:4-10).

"The Lord . . . is patient . . . not wishing for any to
perish but for all to come to repentance." This is still
God's attitude, just as it was His attitude toward the
people of Canaan. It has been His attitude toward the
whole world since the day Adam and Eve sinned in the
Garden. Through Abraham and Israel, and in these last
days through Jesus Christ, He has been reaching out to
all men. His long-suffering is obvious.

Jesus Christ is still waiting for people to turn to Him.
He is delaying His return to earth, because He desires
that all men be saved. Obviously, not all will turn to
Him. But some will—just like Rahab and her family.

What about you? Have you personally received Jesus
Christ to be your Saviour from sin? If you would like to
receive Him and His forgiveness, pray this prayer with
sincerity and He will indeed give you eternal life:

*"Father, I,_____have sinned. Though my sins
are not as great as the Canaanites of old, I am still sinful
and separated from God. Thank you for dying for my
sins. I now receive you as my own personal Saviour from
sin. Thank you for accepting me, for saving me and for
giving me eternal life."*

There is also a tremendous lesson in this story for
Christians. God uses people to reach people. And within
His plan there are five dimensions to His missionary
strategy:

The first dimension is "being." What "we are" as a
local body of believers is foundational to having an effective missionary outreach into our local community.
"Being" what Christ commanded and prayed for in
John's Gospel should serve as a dynamic bridge to the

world. Our love for one another (see John 13:34,35), bearing the fruit of righteousness (see John 15:8) and unity (see John 17:20-23) all attract non-Christians, first to us, and then to Jesus Christ, the One who has made us what we are. In many respects this was also God's plan for the nation Israel in the Old Testament.

The second dimension is "going." Though "being" is foundational and essential for effective community outreach for the local church, it is only the beginning point. Body visibility only lays the groundwork for personal verbalization. Non-Christians can only understand and comprehend the gospel as they hear it explained. How much are you involved in "going" to those who need to hear the message?

The third dimension is "sending." Not all Christians are called upon to leave their homes and communities in order to be missionaries or evangelists. In fact, most of the New Testament Christians who were converted to Christ from various pagan communities never left those communities. Rather, God's plan was that they remain where they were and become a dynamic corporate witness to the rest of their immediate community. However, His plan also was that there would be those who would go out from among them to personally carry the message of the gospel into the community and to the ends of the earth, supported by these Christians both in prayer and finances. How much are you involved in "sending" others to preach the gospel to those who have not heard?

The fourth dimension is "giving." Financially supporting those who desire to serve Jesus Christ full-time as missionaries is just as much a part of carrying out the Great Commission as "going." From a Christian point of view we cannot conscientiously send people out without meeting their physical needs and providing them with financial security. How much are you utilizing your financial resources to achieve God's purposes in this world? Are you giving systematically, proportionally, and cheerfully (see 2 Cor. 9:6,7)?

The last, but not least dimension is the missionary activity called "praying." Christians are, of course, to pray about many things—about *all* things (see Phil. 4:6). But there are many New Testament examples that tell us we are to pray for those who represent us as missionaries. How faithful are you in praying for those you support and have helped to send out?

LIFE RESPONSE

Consider the following questions to help you evaluate the extent to which you are helping to carry out the Great Commission of Jesus Christ:

1. To what extent am I contributing to the dynamic body life and witness of my church?

2. To what extent am I personally sharing Christ with non-Christians?

3. To what extent am I encouraging others to serve in the area of missionary outreach?

4. To what extent am I financially supporting missions?

5. To what extent am I praying for those who go?

FOLLOW-UP PROJECT

Meditate on Romans 1:16-32; 5:1-9.

Notes

1. This is not a new phenomenon in the Old Testament. For example, God also appeared to Abraham in human form and conveyed a special message. See Genesis 18:1-33.
2. For more detail regarding archaeological discoveries, see Howard F. Vos, *Archaeology in Bible Lands* (Chicago: Moody Press), pp. 179-181. See also Jack Finegan, *Light from the Ancient Past* (London: Oxford University Press), vol. 1, pp. 156-159.

ACHAN'S SIN

Achan's Disobedience (Josh. 7:1)
Israel's Defeat (Josh. 7:2-5)
Joshua's Dismay (Josh. 7:6-9)
The Lord's Direction (Josh. 7:10-15)
Achan Is Discovered (Josh. 7:16-21)
The Result—Death (Josh. 7:22-26)[1]

As a young person growing up in my particular religious background, my view of God was somewhat distorted. Unfortunately, I saw Him more as a God of wrath than a God of love. The fact is that the accounts of His long-suffering and patience with the weaknesses of mankind are far more prevalent in the Bible than accounts of His judgments. But there are times when His patience ran out and He administered severe punishment for sin. This is particularly true when there was flagrant disobedience in the full light of His divine revelation. In these situations, to allow the sin to go unnoticed and unpunished would have caused the masses to lose respect for His Word. The children of Israel had that natural tendency anyway.

Achan's sin illustrates this truth dramatically. Though it is a sobering story, it is one the children of Israel never forgot. And any thinking Christian who reads it carefully can only thank God for the blood of Christ that keeps on cleansing us from all sin (see 1 John 1:9).

The miracle at Jericho was a great victory for Joshua, for the Israelites and, most important, for the God of Israel! Humanly speaking there was no way to explain the event. It was indeed another miracle—equal in intensity, drama and divine significance to their escape from Egypt via the Red Sea and their entrance into Canaan through the Jordan River. Jericho was the first city to fall under the judgment of God. The next would be Ai, another Canaanite city that lay about 10 miles west of Jericho. Whatever fear and ambivalence the children of Israel may have felt when they first approached Jericho faded away in the light of their astounding victory.

But lurking in the shadows was a serious problem—a problem of sin that would soon turn the Israelites' spirit of confidence into internal anxiety, emotional confusion and doubt. A man by the name of Achan violated some of God's specific instructions regarding the spoils of Jericho. Consequently, Israel was about to experience a humiliating defeat.

ACHAN'S DISOBEDIENCE (Josh. 7:1)

When the Lord initially gave Joshua instructions regarding the way they were to attack and capture Jericho, He had stated specifically that the entire city was "under the ban." This meant that everything and everyone in the city must be destroyed and burned with fire. In addition to Rahab and her family, there was only one exception: "All the silver and gold and articles of bronze and iron" were to be considered "holy to the Lord" and were to "go into the treasury of the Lord" (Josh. 6:19).

Achan, an Israelite from the tribe of Judah, intentionally and deliberately disregarded God's command. Secretly he "took some of the things under the ban" and hid them in his tent. Consequently, God's anger "burned against the sons of Israel" (7:1).

For God to place people and things "under the ban" was not a new phenomenon in Israel. In fact, it was written into the laws given to Israel at Sinai (see Lev. 27:29). And when Moses reviewed the law prior to their entrance into Canaan, he explained to Israel and warned them regarding the ban. Thus we read:

> And the Lord your God will clear away these nations before you little by little .... And He will deliver their kings into your hand so that you shall make their name perish from under heaven; no man will be able to stand before you until you have destroyed them. The graven images of their gods you are to burn with fire; you shall not covet the silver or the gold that is on them, nor take it for yourselves, lest you be snared by it, for it is an abomination to the Lord your God. And you shall not bring an abomination into your house, and become a devoted thing like it [that is, banned]; you shall utterly detest it and you shall utterly abhor it, for it is a devoted thing [that is, it is banned] (Deut. 7:22,24-26).

God placed Jericho and everything in it under the ban. In full awareness of God's warning through Moses and now through Joshua regarding what would happen to him and his whole household, Achan took some of the silver and the gold and fine clothes from Jericho and concealed them in his tent. Achan flagrantly, and in the full light of God's revelation, violated His holy law! In God's sight it was an act of idolatry and wickedness that must be punished.

No one in Israel knew about Achan's disobedience except the Lord Himself. And what happened next in this story is rather ironical.

ISRAEL'S DEFEAT (Josh. 7:2-5)

Following Israel's tremendous victory in Jericho, Joshua took immediate steps to conquer the city of Ai. He sent some men to spy out the city. When they returned, they were very positive about the potential victory. Their report to Joshua radiated confidence and self-assurance: "Do not let all the people go up," they said. "Only about two or three thousand men need go up to Ai; do not make all the people toil up there, for they are few" (7:3).

Unfortunately, Joshua took these men at their word! He sent a small band of men to capture this city. And to his amazement, the men of Ai struck back and defeated Israel.

Joshua and all the children of Israel were nonplussed. They couldn't believe their eyes. They were so frightened that their hearts "melted and became as water" (7:5).

What happened? No one really knew! The root problem of course was hidden sin in the camp of Israel. But there were some surface problems too. Though Achan was primarily at fault, there were others in Israel who were guilty of taking matters into their own hands. Israel had come off of an unbelievable victory—a spiritual high, if you will. And in their reactions you can easily detect their feelings of pride and arrogance. In fact, the men who were sent to spy out Ai were so sure of themselves they didn't take time to get all the facts. They woefully misjudged the number of armed warriors in Ai! And most tragic, they failed to remember that it was God who had given them the victory in Jericho—not their great wisdom and human strategies.

Have you ever faced this kind of problem in your life as a Christian? I have! I am most vulnerable following some great accomplishment or victory. How easy it is at those times to misjudge, to become overly self-assured, to rely solely upon my own strengths and abilities! And frequently God has to teach me—through allowing defeat in my life—that I must maintain an intricate balance between having confidence in myself and continually trusting in God to guide me and help me to discern His perfect will. Unfortunately, I sometimes learn that lesson "reaching up to touch bottom."

How quickly we can stumble and fall. And often it happens when we *feel* the most successful in our Christian experience. And when it happens it's sometimes difficult to understand the problem or how to approach the situation with spiritual perspective. This was Joshua's problem, too!

JOSHUA'S DISMAY (Josh. 7:6-9)

When Israel was defeated by the men from Ai, Joshua was caught totally off guard! Even as a mature man of God, his emotions quickly took over. Though outwardly he humbled himself before the Lord—"he tore his clothes and fell to the earth"—in reality, he was more concerned about his own feelings of dismay than he was to get to the root of the problem. This is obvious from his prayer:

> *And Joshua said, "Alas, O Lord God, why didst Thou ever bring this people over the Jordan, only to deliver us into the hand of the Amorites, to destroy us? If only we had been willing to dwell beyond the Jordan! Oh Lord, what can I say since Israel has turned their back before their enemies? For the Canaanites and all the inhabitants of the land will hear of it, and they will surround us and cut off our*

111

*name from the earth. And what wilt Thou do
for Thy great name?"* (7:7-9).

It is obvious that Joshua had lost perspective. In this
moment of defeat he quickly forgot God's promise that
He was going to give them the land. Had not the Lord
just instructed Joshua to circumcise the sons of Israel as
a sign of that promise? Had they not just remembered
their great deliverance from Egypt with the Passover?
And what about the memorial stones? And most of all,
what about Jericho? Was it possible that God so quickly
had forsaken them?

Joshua's reactions of course reveal that he was human
—just like you and me. There is a fine line between
feelings of success and feelings of failure. One moment
we can be elated with our achievements. And a short
time later we can be depressed over our failures. And
when depressed and dismayed, we often lose sight of
God's overall plan for our lives—His promises, His
previous victories and His divine presence with us! And
often God has to deal with us just as He did with Joshua.
He has to remind us of the facts!

THE LORD'S DIRECTION (Josh. 7:10-15)

Though Joshua's emotions were real, in many respects they were surface feelings! Joshua was too mature a man to go down in deep despair and defeat! God
knew he was feeling sorry for himself. Consequently
God dealt with him at that level! "Rise up! Why is it
that you have fallen on your face?" (7:10).

With this question the Lord implied that Joshua
should have known what was wrong. Had Joshua
stopped to think for a moment, he logically would have
concluded that someone had violated God's law regarding the ban on Jericho. Thus the Lord answered His own
question directly and to the point!

Israel has sinned, and they have also trans-

gressed My covenant which I commanded them. And they have even taken some of the things under the ban and have both stolen and deceived. Moreover, they have also put them among their own things. Therefore the sons of Israel cannot stand before their enemies; they turn their backs before their enemies, for they have become accursed. I will not be with you any more unless you destroy the things under the ban from your midst (7:11,12).

To solve the problem the Lord gave Joshua some very unique instructions. Rather than immediately identifying Achan and those involved with him, the Lord spelled out a specific method for discovering the culprit. First, *all* the children of Israel were to consecrate themselves before the Lord (see 7:13). All of them were to search their hearts, for in reality they were all guilty of pride and having failed to trust God following their victory at Jericho.

Next the Lord revealed the procedure for discovering Achan:

In the morning then you shall come near by your tribes. And it shall be that the tribe which the Lord takes by lot shall come near by families, and the family which the Lord takes shall come near by households, and the household which the Lord takes shall come near man by man (7:14).

ACHAN IS DISCOVERED (Josh. 7:16-21)

Think for a moment why God used this tactic. Why didn't He just identify Achan and the others involved? Personally I believe there are two reasons. First, God wanted Israel to observe the process and to never forget! As each lot fell and as each *tribe, family* and *household* was identified, all Israel would have a chance to think hard and long about the seriousness of violating God's commandments! Short memories often need dramatic experiences!

Second, I believe God, in His divine love and mercy, was once again offering a way of escape to a man who had woefully disobeyed Him. Had Achan immediately confessed and truly repented of his sin, he and his whole household *may* have been spared! It would be consistent with God's nature to do this, for years later He pardoned David the king of Israel who committed two horrible sins which should have brought him death. But because of David's repentant heart the Lord spared him.

In Achan's situation it seems that God was giving him time—just as He did for the people of Jericho. First, his tribe was identified—then, his family, and finally his household! And then the lot fell on him! *After all this*, Achan confessed his sin! His back was against the wall. He had no choice. His confession was forced! It was too late—just as it will be for many some day when *every* knee shall bow before God and acknowledge who He is (see Phil. 2:10,11).

THE RESULT—DEATH (Josh. 7:22-26)

The end of this story is tragic! Achan and his family and everything he owned, including what he had stolen, were completely destroyed and burned with fire. Because Achan identified himself with the ban God placed on Jericho, he and his whole household were brought under the same judgment.

LESSONS FOR TODAY

This Old Testament passage is one of the most sobering in all the Bible. It teaches us that God indeed is a holy God. Though He is patient and long-suffering, He cannot persistently tolerate sin, especially when it is flagrantly committed in the light of His full and direct revelation. In other words, the more light we have, the more He holds us responsible and accountable to live up to that light.

This is dramatically illustrated in the life of Achan. God revealed Himself again and again, not only through visible signs and miracles but by direct commands. Years before He warned Israel against this kind of sin, that to indulge in it would bring judgment on an entire household. Just to make sure they understood the seriousness of this law, God reviewed this matter for Israel just before they entered Jericho (see Josh. 6:18). And it was in the full light of God's direct warning that Achan disobeyed God! In many respects it would be as serious as walking into the holy of holies in the Tabernacle and pushing the Ark of the Covenant to the ground, replacing it with a pagan idol. It was a very serious form of idolatry.

It must be pointed out that the Bible records very few times when God breaks through with this kind of judgment. But when He does, it falls on people who have willfully disobeyed God in the full light of His revealed power.

It seems that this is what happened to Ananias and Sapphira in the New Testament. They had experienced the miracle of Pentecost. They had personally witnessed the coming of the Holy Spirit with tongues of fire and with a mighty rushing wind throughout Jerusalem. They had seen the miracles performed by the apostles. And in the midst of all of these dramatic events wrought by God, Satan caused them "to lie to the Holy Spirit." Consequently, they were severely judged by God. Both of them died on the spot! And when it happened, "great fear came upon the whole church, and upon all who heard" about it (Acts 5:11).

Both of these stories teach all of us an important lesson. Yes, God is holy and He hates sin, but the primary lesson is that in a very real sense we are all under the ban—for we "all have sinned and fall short of the glory of God" (Rom. 3:23). Again Paul states, "There is none righteous, not even one" (Rom. 3:10). This is why God instituted the sacrifice in the Old Testament. This is why He eventually sent His Son, Jesus Christ, to die for the sins of the world. When we receive Jesus Christ— when we believe that He died for us personally, He justifies us and makes us righteous in His sight.

LIFE RESPONSE

Do you know Christ personally? Can you say, "If I,_____, died tonight, I know I would go to heaven and be with Christ forever?" If you can say this, write your name in the blank. If you cannot and you want to know Christ, sincerely pray the following prayer:

"Father, I know that I am a sinner. I know I have failed you. I receive your Son, Jesus Christ, to be my Saviour from sin. Thank you for the gift of salvation."

Now, go back and write your name in the blank.

There is a question Christians also must ask themselves. "Am I a believer who is willingly and deliberately living in sin?" If you are, God is displeased. He wants us to live holy and righteous lives.

NOTE: If you are constantly living in conscious sin—if you are willingly violating God's laws—and if you are truly a son of God, He, as a loving father, will discipline you (see Heb. 12:7-11). Are you being disciplined? If so, thank God, for you are a son! Acknowledge your sins and claim His forgiveness in Jesus Christ (see 1 John 1:9). If you are living in sin and are not being disciplined in your conscience and other areas of your life, then perhaps you need to reevaluate your relationship to Jesus Christ. Is it real?

Remember not to take advantage of God's grace. Because He does not deal with you immediately does not mean that He never will. Don't forget that the general reactions of the Lord are ones of patience and long-suffering.

Take a few moments to reflect on your life. If you have just received Jesus Christ as your personal Saviour, thank Him for His marvelous gift to you. Ask Him to help you grow in your Christian life.

If you are a Christian, and you know there are things in your life that are not proper for a Christian, take this moment to confess your sins to Him. Receive the forgiveness He has promised. Then write out a goal for your life in a particular area that has been defeating you. Ask God to help you carry out this goal. Remember the words of Paul in Philippians 4:13: "I can do all things through Him who strengthens me."

FOLLOW-UP PROJECT

Memorize the following verses:

No temptation has overtaken you but such as is common to man; and God is faithful, who will not allow you to be tempted beyond what you are able; but with the temptation will provide the way of escape also, that you may be able to endure it (1 Cor. 10:13).

If we confess our sins, He is faithful and righteous to forgive us our sins and to cleanse us from all unrighteousness (1 John 1:9).

Note:

1. The outline in this chapter was developed by Dr. Donald Campbell, academic dean at Dallas Theological Seminary. I seldom borrow outlines, either in my teaching or writing, since I like to create my own through personal research and study. However, I feel that Dr. Campbell's outline is so superb and representative of what is recorded in Joshua chapter 7 that I use it to present this material. (Used by permission.)

VICTORY AT AI

Reassurance for Joshua (Josh. 8:1,2a)
Instructions to Joshua (Josh. 8:2b-17)
Victory Over Ai (Josh. 8:18-29)

There's a divine mystery I'll never understand, at least while I'm living on this earth. But I know it is true. God can take the results of human weakness and, if we let Him, make them work together for good (see Rom. 8:28).

How frequently I've seen this happen in my own life. Some of the greatest lessons I've learned resulted from my own mistakes or the mistakes others made that have touched my life.

We see this truth illustrated in this chapter. God took the results of Israel's sin and used it to give them victory at Ai.

The humiliating defeat over Israel by the inhabitants

119

of Ai and the tragic events surrounding the household of Achan left Joshua a fearful and brokenhearted man. Not only was it horribly difficult to have to face his responsibility to issue the order to execute Achan and his family, but surrounding him were thousands of discouraged and frustrated Israelites. Gloom and despair permeated the whole camp of Israel.

How quickly it all happened! Ever since the Lord spoke to Joshua following Moses' death, reassuring him of His blessings on him as the new leader of Israel, Joshua had responded with courage and inner strength. He took God at His word. His fears dissipated and his faith was strong. He triumphantly guided the children of Israel across Jordan. He boldly led the army of Israel against Jericho, *knowing* they would be victorious.

But suddenly, within hours, Joshua found himself experiencing the old frustrations and anxieties. His triumphant faith turned to immobilizing fear. He felt defeated and in despair. He saw no way out. A black cloud of depression gripped his soul and hovered over all Israel.

But God had not forsaken Joshua *or* His people. He would not and could not! He had promised them the land if they would obey Him. And because Joshua carried out His commands regarding Achan, "the Lord turned from the fierceness of His anger" (Josh. 7:26). Immediately God took steps to reassure Joshua that He indeed was with him and would help him lead Israel on to further victories.

REASSURANCE FOR JOSHUA (Josh. 8:1,2a)

Though Joshua was not responsible for the sin that led to Israel's defeat, he was not above reproach in the way he handled the maneuver against Ai. It appears that he took matters into his own hands rather than consulting the Lord for specific directions. Also his response to their defeat reflected less than the mature man of God that he was. In a moment of weakness he reverted to his old ways. Thus, Joshua's heavenly Father was rather frontal in dealing with his attitudes and actions (see Josh. 7:10,11).

But once God dealt with the original cause of the problem, He quickly reassured Joshua that He had not forsaken him or Israel:

> *Do not fear or be dismayed. Take all the people of war with you and arise, go up to Ai; see, I have given into your hand the king of Ai, his people, his city, and his land. And you shall do to Ai and its king just as you did to Jericho and its king* (8:1,2a).

It's obvious from the Lord's comprehensive statement that He wanted Joshua to feel secure. Thus the Lord told him He would give him total victory—over the king, the people, the city and the land.

Note also that God's words of encouragement to Joshua to "not fear or be dismayed" were the very same words Moses spoke years before to the people in Kadesh-Barnea before he sent the 12 men to spy out the land of Canaan (see Deut. 1:21). And they were also the same words Moses spoke to Joshua 40 years later when he turned the reins of leadership over to this young man following Israel's wilderness experience (see Deut. 31: 8). At this moment in Joshua's life, following this humiliating defeat, God *specifically* reminded Joshua of His promise. Achan's sin, serious as it was, did not mean the Lord had forsaken Israel. Nor did Joshua's immature response mean that God would not continue to use him as His chosen leader of the children of Israel.

To make His point even more reassuring, the Lord told Joshua that Israel would be able to capture Ai *just as they had captured Jericho*. Their strategy would be different, but the results would be the same. Israel would emerge victorious.

There was one other difference. When they captured Jericho, everything was placed under the ban. But at Ai, the Lord promised that they would be able to take of the spoils of the city (see Josh. 8:2). How ironic! Had Achan waited, had he not allowed greed and selfishness to take over in his life, he would have been able to take all he wanted and needed at Ai. Sadly, he moved out ahead of the Lord, took matters into his own hands, violated God's law and brought judgment on himself and his whole family.

INSTRUCTIONS TO JOSHUA (Josh. 8:2b-17)

After reassuring Joshua that he had not forsaken Israel, the Lord told him how he was to capture Ai. They were to "set an ambush for the city behind it" (8:2b).[1]

As you read through verses 2-17 in Joshua 8 there are some unique problems that surface regarding the specific details of the strategy. However, the following seems to be the most consistent explanation, although there is a difference of opinion among competent Old Testament scholars.

First, Joshua selected 30 key men, "valiant warriors, and sent them out at night" to camp behind the city of Ai (on the west side). These men, highly qualified, comprised a commando unit that was to eventually enter the city and set it on fire.[2]

Behind this contingent of men there was another ambuscade comprising 5,000 men (see 8:12). When the proper signal was given by Joshua, they were to follow the 30 commandos into the city as the rear guard, adding support to the ambush (see 8:13).[3]

In order to set the stage for this surprise attack Joshua used a deceptive tactic. He and a number of other men in Israel went up to Ai following the same route as those who were previously defeated. They camped overnight in the valley north of Ai in full view of the enemy. And when the king of Ai saw what was happening, he ordered his own army to attack Israel just as they had done previously. Since he knew nothing of the Israelites who were waiting to attack from the west, he held none of his men back (see 8:14).

The plan worked perfectly. Joshua and his men "pretended to be beaten before them, and fled by the way of the wilderness. And all the people who were in the city were called together to pursue them, and they pursued Joshua, and were drawn away from the city. So not a man was left in Ai or Bethel who had not gone out after Israel, and they left the city unguarded and pursued Israel" (8:15-17). It was then that Joshua signaled the attack from the rear.[4]

VICTORY OVER AI (Josh. 8:18-29)

At just the right moment the Lord told Joshua to raise his javelin into the air. This was the signal to attack Ai from the rear. Evidently men stationed at various distances formed a visual line that "radioed" the message to the commando units. And attack they did! They entered Ai without resistance and "quickly set the city on fire" (8:19).

Imagine the surprise and fear that gripped the men of Ai. When they looked back they saw billows of smoke rising into the sky. The whole city was in flames. And before they could gather their wits Joshua and his men, who were feigning retreat, suddenly turned and attacked. The 5,000 men who had followed the initial commando unit into the city from the west moved right on through the city and attacked the men of Ai from behind. Consequently, they "were trapped in the midst of Israel" and were utterly destroyed (8:22).

Next, Israel's army reentered the city and brought God's judgment upon the entire population, just as they had done in Jericho. "And all who fell that day, both men and women, were 12,000—all the people of Ai" (8:25).

The king, however, was taken captive and delivered to Joshua. Later, he was executed and buried beneath a pile of stones at the entrance to the city (see 8:23,29). Ai had fallen! And once again God proved Himself faithful to Israel. Not only had they destroyed their enemies, but they received a reward as well. They were allowed to take "the cattle and the spoil of that city as plunder for themselves" (8:27).

LESSONS FOR TODAY

There are at least two very clear and practical truths that stand out in this passage which are consistently relevant even for Christians living in the twentieth-century world.

First, God will never forsake His children, no matter how much they have forsaken Him. Though Israel had violated God's law and though Joshua had responded to God's discipline immaturely, God did not forsake them as they thought He would. True, the Lord eventually judged Israel's persistent disobedience by scattering them "from one end of the earth to the other" (Deut. 28:64). But it is also true that God will ultimately keep His promise to Israel in spite of their utter failure. He will gather them from "the ends of the earth" and eventually bring them into the land which their fathers possessed (see Deut, 30:45).

God's promise to be with His children is even more striking and binding in the New Testament. We read in Hebrews 13:5: "For He Himself has said, 'I will never desert you, nor will I ever forsake you.' " And when the Lord gave His followers the Great Commission He promised, "And lo, I am with you *always*, even to the end of the age" (Matt. 28:20).

The apostle Paul believed and taught this truth without qualification. Listen to his words in his letter to the Roman Christians:

> *What then shall we say to these things? If God is for us, who is against us? ... Who shall separate us from the love of Christ? Shall tribulation, or distress, or persecution, or famine, or nakedness or peril, or sword? ... But in all these things we overwhelmingly conquer through Him who loved us. For I am convinced that neither death, nor life, nor angels, nor principalities, nor things present, nor things to come, nor powers, nor height, nor depth, nor any other created thing, shall be able to separate us from the love of God, which is in Christ Jesus our Lord* (Rom. 8:31,35,37-39).

Obviously, God is displeased and disappointed when we sin against Him, when we fail to do His will. But no sin or failure can ever separate us spiritually from God. He promised us *eternal* life and He cannot lie, no matter how much we fail Him.

On the other hand, the Bible teaches that no Christian who knows God's will and who has experienced God's saving grace can continue to live in flagrant sin without being disciplined. Hopefully, he will eventually acknowledge that sin and turn from it (see Heb. 12:11). As we said in our previous lesson, a true child of God *will* be disciplined by his heavenly Father. If we experience no discipline, the Bible states explicitly that we "are illegitimate children and not sons" (Heb. 12:8).

What about you? Are you flagrantly living outside the will of God? Perhaps you believe the Lord has forsaken you. Rest assured He has not. He is waiting for you to turn from your sins and to experience His forgiveness (see 1 John 1:9). Perhaps your feelings of aloneness and your sense of being forsaken are in themselves a result

125

of your sin. Your feelings of alienation can be part of the disciplinary process God has allowed in your life to cause you to once again turn to Him and walk in His will. God is patiently waiting for you to respond to His unconditional love and grace.

On the one hand we must never take advantage of that love; on the other hand, we must never misjudge it. It is always available, no matter how much we fail Him. Accept His forgiveness and in the process, forgive yourself. Then live in the joy of that forgiveness constantly conforming your life to the life of Jesus Christ.

Second, God can take the mistakes His children make and can turn them into positive results. This is what the Lord did with Israel's mistake in trying to attack Ai when they were unprepared both spiritually and militarily. He used the very strategy that had originally brought defeat to Israel in order to eventually deceive and trap the men of Ai.

Only God can take our mistakes and the results of those mistakes and make them "work together for good" (Rom. 8:28). This does not mean that we will not experience the negative effects of our failures—just as Israel did. Thirty-six choice men lost their lives because they walked out of the will of God (see Josh. 7:5). Furthermore, fear and anxiety gripped their hearts. Morale was at a low ebb. They doubted God's love and forgot His promises.

But God changed all that for Israel. And He can do it for us, too! If we let Him, He can turn our blunders into blessings.

LIFE RESPONSE

Read the following paraphrase of Romans 8:28-39. Personalize this message from the Lord by mentally or literally writing your name in each blank. Then thank God for these reassuring promises.

*And we know that God causes all things to work together for good to*_____ *who loves God, to*_____*who is called according to His purpose. For He fore-knew*_____*and He also predes-tined*_____*to become conformed to the image of His Son, that He might be the first-born among many brethren. And when He predestined*_____*He also called*_____*;and whom He called, He also justified; and*_____ *whom He justified He also glorified. What then shall we say to these things? If God is for* _____*who is against me? He who did not spare His own Son, but delivered Him up for*_____*, how will He not also with Him freely give*_____ *all things? Who will bring a charge against* _____*? God is the one who justi-fies; who is the one who condemns? Christ Jesus is He who died, yes, rather who was raised, who is at the right hand of God, who also intercedes for*_____*. Who shall separate*_____*from the love of Christ? Shall tribulation, or dis-tress, or persecution, or famine, or nakedness, or peril, or sword? ... But in all these things* _____*can overwhelmingly con-quer through Him who loved me. For I am convinced that neither death, nor life, nor an-gels, nor principalities, nor things present, nor things to come, nor powers, nor height, nor depth, nor any other created thing, shall be able to separate*_____*from the love of God, which is in Christ Jesus our Lord.* (Rom. 8:28-39, paraphrase)

FOLLOW-UP PROJECT

Memorize Romans 8:28:

> *And we know that God causes all things to work together for good to those who love God, to those who are called according to His purpose.*

Notes

1. At this point it is difficult to determine how much detail God actually gave Joshua regarding *how* to carry out this ambush. The text simply records the simple statement by the Lord to "set an ambush for the city behind it" (Josh. 8:2b). The author then moved quickly to a description of the process as Joshua explained his strategy to the people.

It is my personal opinion that the Lord gave these specific details to Joshua, and he in turn repeated them to the people. This would be consistent with what the Lord did regarding how to capture Jericho. Furthermore, Joshua needed this kind of security at this time in his life. And *specific* instructions from the Lord regarding how to capture Ai would certainly contribute to that needed security.

2. Irving L. Jensen gives the following explanation regarding the number of men chosen in Joshua 8:3: "The size of this group is indicated by the text as 30,000 men, which appears to be an unusually large contingent for such a secret maneuver as ambush close to the city. One plausible answer to the problem is that the text should read 'thirty officers.' This suggestion is made by R.E.D. Clark, who points out that the Hebrew word *elep*, translated 'thousand,' can also be translated as 'chief' or 'officer,' as it is translated in other passages (cf. 1 Chron. 12:23-27; 2 Chron. 13:3,17; 17:14-19). If this were the case, then the thirty-man group was a highly selected commando unit, assigned to enter the vacated city and burn it. This view may better explain also the description of the contingent as chosen for being 'mighty men of valor' —more meaningful to a thirty-man group than to a 30,000-man unit." Irving L. Jensen, *Joshua Rest—Land Won*, Everyman's Bible Commentary (Chicago: Moody Press, 1966), p. 72.

3. There are two basic ways to solve the textual problem in this passage. One is to equate the 30,000 men with the 5,000 men who are lying in ambush and explain the numerical discrepancy as a scribal error. This is feasible since these men are described as being located "between Bethel and Ai on the west side of Ai" (Josh. 8:9,12). The second explanation is that there were two groups of men lying in wait to ambush. The first group was comprised of 30 commandos who were *closer to the city* (see Josh. 8:4), backed by a second contingency of 5,000 (see note 2 for the explanation regarding the 30,000 figure given in Josh. 8:3). Personally, I favor the second explanation which is the one I've developed in this chapter.

4. Evidently the king of Ai secured help from the king of Bethel in case of the second attack by Israel. Consequently, those who pursued Israel were from both cities (see Josh. 8:17).

JOSHUA'S OBEDIENCE TO MOSES' COMMAND

Joshua Builds an Altar to the Lord (Josh. 8:30,31)
Joshua Reviews the Law of Moses (Josh. 8:32-35)
A More Careful Look (Deut. 27:1-26)

In order to get our attention, the Holy Spirit often directed scriptural authors to use sharp contrasts as a literary technique in recording various events that transpired throughout biblical history. This is what we see in Joshua 8 following Israel's unusual victory at Ai. In fact, the contrast is so sharp, not only from a literary standpoint but also in geographical setting, that some critics of the Bible believe that events recorded in this passage are out of sequence and were added by another author. Unfortunately they miss the important purpose the Lord had in mind when He directed the author of the book of Joshua to suddenly transport Israel and the reader from Ai to Mount Ebal in Shechem. But this geographical contrast only forms a dramatic backdrop against which a *spiritual contrast* stands out clearly on the pages of holy writ. What was that contrast?

JOSHUA BUILDS AN ALTAR TO THE LORD
(Josh. 8:30,31)

The final event recorded regarding Israel's victory over Ai was the execution of the king of the city. His body was buried at the gate of Ai, under "a great heap of stones" (8:29). Immediately following this statement we read:

> *Then Joshua built an altar to the Lord, the God of Israel, in Mount Ebal* (8:30).

The contrast is striking! At the gate of a pagan city that now lay defeated and desolate was the body of a pagan king, memorialized with a pile of stones, symbolizing the futility of worshiping the false gods of the Canaanites. And at Mt. Ebal—in the very center of the land of Canaan—we see Joshua constructing an altar (also a pile of stones) to the God of Israel, symbolizing the blessings and protection that come from worshiping the one true God, "the God of Israel."[1]

There's more here, however, than just a contrast between paganism and Judaism—between the results of following false gods and the one true God. Joshua had learned a very important lesson based on his personal relationship with God and in his relationship to Israel as their political, military and—most important—their spiritual leader. He had experienced a great and rewarding victory at Jericho (see Josh. 6), followed by a humiliating and traumatic defeat at Ai (see Josh. 7). Though Joshua was not directly responsible for Israel's failure, his initial response to the crisis (see 7:6-9) served as a rather painful reminder that it is very easy to quickly forget God's promises and the conditions He attaches to those promises. This is particularly true during times of great successes and victories. And God's method for reminding Joshua of His initial conversation with this new leader of Israel was to allow him to experience some of the old fears and anxieties that had plagued him when Moses' mantle fell on his shoulders.

Don't misunderstand! God was not responsible for Achan's sin *nor* Israel's failure. As only the Lord can do, He simply took what was human failure and weakness and used it for good, particularly in the life of Israel. In the midst of this crisis, Joshua experienced the old fears that had gripped him following Moses' death. With those fears came a reminder of what God had promised in the midst of his human weakness: "Be strong and courageous, for *you shall give this people possession of the land which I swore to their fathers to give them*" (Josh. 1:6; see also Josh. 8:1,2).

Not only did Joshua's emotional and spiritual crisis remind him of God's promises but also of God's conditions for success—five direct commands that relate specifically to what was about to happen at Mount Ebal. Remember? In those early days of trauma following Moses' death God said, "You *shall* give this people possession of the land" (1:6). *But* here were God's conditions:

First, "Be careful to do according to *all the law*" (1:7a).

Second, "Do not turn from it to the right or to the left" (1:7b).

Third, "This book of the law shall not depart from your mouth" (1:8a).

Fourth, "You shall meditate on it day and night" (1:8b).

Fifth, "Be careful to do according to all that is written in it" (1:8c).

This is why,

> *Joshua built an altar to the Lord, the God*
> *of Israel, in Mount Ebal, just as Moses the*

*servant of the Lord had commanded the sons
of Israel, as it is written in the Book of the Law
of Moses, an altar of uncut stones, on which
no man had wielded an iron tool; and they
offered burnt offerings on it to the Lord, and
sacrificed peace offerings* (Josh. 8:30,31).

It is clear from the flow of events recorded thus far in
the book of Joshua that what happened at Mount Ebal
following the victory at Ai forms a perfect continuity in
the life of both Joshua and Israel. Their defeat and
subsequent victory motivated them to go back to the
"drawing board," back to God's basics. Before they ever
entered the land Moses told them specifically to build
an altar to the Lord at Mount Ebal (see Deut. 27:4-7).
You see, they were obeying God's command. And in the
process they were also reviewing God's Word to make
sure they would continue "to do according to *all* the law
. . . according to *all* that is written in it." Joshua, particularly, did not want to face another Ai and the same kind
of tragic events surrounding Achan's household and Israel's humiliating defeat.

JOSHUA REVIEWS THE LAW OF MOSES
(Josh. 8:32-35)

Not only had Moses instructed Israel to "build an
altar to the Lord" at Mount Ebal, but also to carefully
"review the law of Moses" in the hearing of *all* the
people of Israel. Memories fade, particularly in a primitive culture where there were no Bibles that could be
read regularly. Effective learning was dependent on oral
communication from spiritual leaders. And Moses'
command to the people of Israel was that, once they had
entered Canaan, they were to spend quality time at
Mount Ebal reviewing God's laws (see Deut. 27:1-3).
Thus, we see Joshua doing what Moses commanded.
First, Joshua wrote the law on large stones (see Josh.

8:32). Then "he read all the words of the law" (8:34). In fact,

> *There was not a word of all that Moses had commanded which Joshua did not read before all the assembly of Israel with the women and the little ones and the strangers who were living among them* (8:35).

Here we have an explicit statement regarding Joshua's obedience to God's command in Joshua 1:8:

> *This book of the law shall not depart from your mouth, but you shall meditate on it day and night, so that you may be careful to do according to all that is written in it; for then you will make your way prosperous, and then you will have success.*

A MORE CAREFUL LOOK (Deut. 27:1-26)

This passage in Joshua 8, though very clearly a significant part of the flow of events of Israel's history, is skeletal in nature. And this, it seems, is by design. For the Holy Spirit was primarily concerned that we note clearly the contrast already referred to and the reasons why Joshua moved all of Israel to this unique place in Canaan to worship the Lord and to review His law.

But the events that took place at Mount Ebal are in themselves very dramatic and intriguing. Though it is impossible to reconstruct all the specific details of this story from the historical record in Joshua 8, it is relatively simple to reconstruct most of them when we go back and look at God's initial instruction to Israel through His servant Moses. These details are recorded in Deuteronomy 27.

There were actually two events at Mount Ebal that involved "stones." Moses instructed the people of Israel to "set up for yourself large stones, and coat them with lime and write on them all the words of this law" (Deut.

27:2,3).[2] It was on these stones that Joshua "wrote . . . a copy of the Law of Moses" (Josh. 8:32).

The second set of stones formed the altar upon which the children of Israel offered burnt offerings and peace offerings (see Deut. 27:5-7; Josh. 8:30,31). These were the stones that were taken from the earth in their natural state, evidently to make an altar that was not tainted by man's efforts at refinement. This altar was to reflect as much as possible *God's* creative hand—not man's. And it was on this altar that Israel made atonement for their sins according to God's law and also worshiped the God of Israel with offerings of thanksgiving and praise.[3]

But the most dramatic part of this story is the actual reading of the law of God to the people and their involvement in the process. Joshua's record gives a brief geographical setting for this event (see Josh. 8:33), but again the specific instructions in the book of Deuteronomy fill in some unique details.

Though more reference is made to Mount Ebal in the biblical text, Israel was actually camped in a valley between *two* mountains—Ebal to the north and Gerizim to the south. Half of the tribes were camped closer to Ebal and half were camped closer to Gerizim. The Levitical priests were evidently camped in the lower part of the valley between the two mountains, where they placed the Ark of the Covenant. Though details are vague, it appears that Joshua first read a statement from the law, then the priests repeated it in unison. These men served as a human amplification system. And as their voices echoed through the valley, all Israel responded to each statement by shouting back, "Amen."

Imagine the impact this event had on all the Canaanites who lived in the vicinity of Mount Ebal and Gerizim. Like all the unique and dramatic situations in Israel's life, this event would be reiterated from one end of Canaan to the other.

What is more important than the method God used is the message He conveyed with this method. The means was indeed dramatic and sensational but the message was definite and sobering. Though what is recorded in Deuteronomy 27 is no doubt representative of what was read from the law, it contains sufficient information to reveal God's will regarding the kind of morality and ethics He demanded from His people. Nearly every significant relationship in life is represented in the 12 statements in Deuteronomy 27:15-26.[4]

Though we do not have space to study carefully the nature of these 12 prohibitions recorded in Deuteronomy 27, a casual reading reveals the religious, moral and ethical deterioration that had taken place in the world of that day. This represents a primary reason why God's hand of judgment fell on the Canaanites by means of His people Israel. And if Israel was to be victorious in their battles against "flesh and blood," it was imperative that they be victorious over "the rulers, against the powers, against the world forces of this darkness, against the spiritual forces of wickedness in the heavenly places" (Eph. 6:12). And thus Israel paused in their march against the cities of Canaan both to nurture their personal relationship with God and to review His will for their lives. This in itself is one of the most important lessons that emerges from this passage for those of us who are Christians living in the twentieth-century world.

LESSONS FOR TODAY

First, Christians must take time on a consistent basis to maintain and regain perspective on God's will in their lives. As with Israel there are two aspects to this process: to review the Word of God and to worship and praise.

We must consistently learn and review God's will through His Word. If we're not careful we can get so busy "doing God's work" that we fail to remember what our objectives really are and what instructions God has given to guide us in the process of reaching those objectives. Remember that the Scriptures are the only reliable and absolute source for discovering this kind of information. (See LIFE RESPONSE questions 1,2 and 3.)

We must also consistently nurture our personal relationship with God through worship and communion with Him. Again this involves both the group process and personal meditation and prayer. In fact, it is almost impossible to develop warm meaningful relationships with the Lord if we are not developing warm meaningful relationships with other members of the Body of Christ. Thus, we need both relationships with one another as well as dynamic relationships with God in order to grow spiritually.

Realize, of course, we do not have to offer sacrifices for our sin as Israel did at Mount Ebal. Jesus Christ paid the supreme sacrifice once and for all (see Heb. 10:4-10). But as Christians we are not to forsake "our own assembling together, as is the habit of some"; rather, we are "to stimulate one another to love and good deeds" (Heb. 10:24,25). And we are "to continually offer up a sacrifice of praise to God, that is, the fruit of lips that give thanks to His name" (Heb. 13:15). (See LIFE RESPONSE questions 4 and 5.)

Second, God never promised that He will specifically reveal His will directly to us every time we need to make a decision.

There was a time in my life when I didn't understand how to determine the will of God for my life, particularly in specific matters. One reason is that I didn't understand the freedom God has given me to make decisions within the context of His written revelation, the Word of God. You see, God never promised that He will specifically reveal His will directly to us every time

136

we need to make a decision. Rather, He gives us sufficient information from the Scriptures to help us make proper decisions at any moment in our lives. Furthermore, He gave Christians His Holy Spirit to guide us in interpreting the Scriptures.

Note that even in Old Testament days—a time when God frequently spoke to men by direct revelation—Joshua was responsible to review what God had already revealed to Moses. He was to meditate on the "book of the law"; he was to study it and communicate it to Israel on a regular basis. This is why they met together at Mount Ebal.

If this was true in Joshua's day, how much more so in our day when we have the full written revelation of God in the 66 books of the Bible. Too many Christians are relying on God to reveal Himself directly in the midst of the decision-making process, without realizing that they are responsible to seek His will through what He has already revealed. (See LIFE RESPONSE question 6.)

How can we determine God's will for us today? There are four important considerations in determining God's will.

First, is there any statement in God's written revelation (the Bible) that is in opposition to this decision? For example, God makes it very clear in Scripture that a Christian should not marry a non-Christian. Also, He makes it clear that Christians should not be divorced simply because they are having difficulty with compatibility in some area in their lives. To do either of these would be a violation of His perfect will. There's no way to make Scripture conform to our feelings if our feelings are out of harmony with Scripture.

Second, what do other mature Christians think about this decision? What advice can they give me?

NOTE: Mature Christians who know what the Word of God says and who are living spiritual lives are very

137

important people in helping us determine God's will. That's why we must never forsake the assembling of ourselves together with other Christians. It's often through the functioning Body of Christ that we learn what His will is for our lives.

Third, what factors in the environment point to the fact that this may be a right or wrong decision?

WARNING: Be careful that you do not allow negative circumstances to be a primary factor in deciding for or against a matter. Many times Christians are called upon to circumvent negative circumstances and to break through environmental barriers. The fact that a Christian is having struggles because of negative circumstances does not mean he is out of the will of God in pursuing a particular course of action.

Fourth, how do I feel about this decision?

A SECOND WARNING: Feelings should be considered last. They are very deceptive and may be purely psychological struggles. Any difficult decision with threatening elements creates negative emotions. Imagine what would have happened if Jesus had paid attention to His feelings when He was praying in the Garden? In His humanity He wanted to walk away from the cross. But in spite of His strong negative emotions, He did the will of God.

LIFE RESPONSE

1. Am I taking time out of my busy schedule to review God's will for my life?

2. Is it part of my priority system to include regular Bible reading and Bible study, both with other Christians and by myself?

NOTE: Christians living in the twentieth century are very privileged people. The children of Israel did not have access to the Word of God as we do. They were dependent solely upon spiritual leaders, such as Joshua and the priests, to communicate and review the law of God for them. We have access to both spiritual leaders and to the Scriptures themselves.

3. Am I taking advantage of the opportunities God has given me to discover His will for my life through personal and group Bible study?

4. Am I pausing sufficiently in my busy schedule to meet regularly with Christ's Body in order to develop meaningful relationships with other Christians and with the Lord?

5. Do I pause sufficiently—even in doing God's work —to thank God and praise Him for who He is and what He is doing for me?

6. To what extent am I trying to determine God's will through existential experience rather than through His written Word?

FOLLOW-UP PROJECT

Memorize Proverbs 3:5,6 and Romans 12:1,2. Together these four verses present some very important truths in making decisions that are within God's perfect will:

> *Trust in the Lord with all your heart, and do not lean on your own understanding. In all your ways acknowledge Him, and He will make your paths straight* (Prov. 3:5,6).

> *I urge you therefore, brethren, by the mercies of God, to present your bodies a living and holy sacrifice, acceptable to God, which is your spiritual service of worship. And do not be conformed to this world, but be transformed by the renewing of your mind, that you may prove what the will of God is, that which is good and acceptable and perfect* (Rom. 12: 1,2).

Notes

1. Why did the author of the book of Joshua not record the details of Israel's journey from Ai to Mount Ebal? It seems logical to conclude that he wanted to demonstrate dramatically the sharp contrast between the "pile of stones" at the gate of the city and "the altar" at Ebal. To separate these two events with geographical detail would cause the average reader to miss the impact of this contrast, if not lose sight of it altogether.

2. Archaeologists have discovered slabs of stone in this part of the country as long as seven feet. Coating them with lime would create a white base on which Joshua could write very clearly and completely the law of God. How much of the law was actually written cannot be fully determined from the text of Scripture. It appears however that Joshua was very comprehensive, which would be a possibility even in view of the lengthy nature of God's laws in the first five books of Moses. In fact, archaeologists have discovered inscriptions on rocks or stones similar to the process Joshua used. A case in point is one such discovery at Behistun in Iran, which includes information about three times the length of Deuteronomy.

3. From the Joshua record it is easy to confuse these two sets of stones. A casual reading could lead to the conclusion that the law was written on the altar of stones (see Josh. 8:32). A careful reading, however, especially with the background of the more detailed descriptions in Deuteronomy 27, clearly reveals two sets of stones.

4. The representative nature of these statements are reflected in the fact that only 12 are recorded, obviously related to the fact that there were 12 tribes in Israel.

THE GIBEONITE DECEPTION

The Strategy (Josh. 9:3-13)
The Deception (Josh. 9:14,15)
The Discovery (Josh. 9:16-22)
The Curse (Josh. 9:23-27)

If you're like I am, the times when I am most vulnerable in making errors in judgment come at moments when I least expect it to happen. And one of those moments when it *shouldn't* happen is when I am most aware and sensitive to the Word of God. But this is one of Satan's tactics—to use the very Word of God itself to deceive us.

Satan is a very subtle enemy. If he cannot reach his insidious goals by causing God's children to flagrantly disobey the Word of God, he on occasions will appear as an "angel of light" and actually *use* God's truth to achieve his objectives.

He did this to Joshua and unfortunately this Old Testament leader made a decision that was irreversible. The children of Israel had just reviewed the law of God at Mount Ebal and Mount Gerizim. Everything God had

141

revealed to Moses was carefully copied on stones and then read to the people. In fact, "there was not a word of all that Moses had commanded which Joshua did not read before all the assembly of Israel with the women and the little ones and the strangers who were living among them" (Josh. 8:35).

THE STRATEGY (Josh. 9:3-13)

Following Israel's great victories at Jericho and Ai, many of the kings of Canaan came together to form an alliance against God's people. It appears they took hope in the fact that Ai had at first succeeded in routing Israel. Not understanding, nor wanting to understand, all of the supernatural factors involved in this initial defeat and subsequent victory, they no doubt thought that what they needed to defeat Israel was more men and more swords and spears. After all, they concluded, Ai defeated Israel when their army was small. They lost only after Israel outnumbered them. And from a purely human perspective this kind of thinking makes sense. But from God's perspective it makes no sense at all. And if these kings had analyzed more carefully Israel's victory at Jericho and how it all happened, they would have come to a much different conclusion.

Among those represented in this summit meeting were men from Gibeon who were called Hivites (9:1,7). Gibeon was one of the largest cities in Canaan. Though the city did not have a king like the other cities, Gibeon was just as respected as any other city. In fact, the author of the book of Joshua described Gibeon as "a great city, like one of the royal cities." Furthermore, "it was greater than Ai, and all its men were mighty" (10:2).

Though all of the kings who gathered to form this military alliance agreed that they would stick together in their fight against Joshua and Israel (see 9:2), the Hivites from Gibeon evidently didn't agree. In fact, it appears that as they listened to the kings discuss Israel's victory over Jericho and Ai, they came to a different conclusion (see 9:3). Rather than join in the military attack against Israel, they decided they would come up with a strategy to make peace with Israel—not war.

The Gibeonites' strategy was cunning and perceptive. They knew they could never defeat Israel in war. They understood clearly that their enemy's military resources were supernatural. They could not ignore what had happened in their previous victories. Any military strategist who was thinking at all would have to conclude that Israel's exploits were divinely directed.

Incidentally, the Gibeonites' conclusion is very interesting. Why would they not join the kings of Cannan in their military alliance? Why would their conclusion regarding Israel's capabilities be different? Personally I believe it had something to do with their form of government. As far as we know, they were the only people in Canaan who had a republic. Rather than being ruled by a sovereign king, like all the other Canaanite cities, they were governed by elders who represented the people in government decisions. Consequently, their decisions were based on input from many people. It appears that this input led them to the conclusion that they would be foolhardy to try to defeat Israel, even if *all* the other cities in Canaan joined in the attack.

This conclusion was accurate. But unfortunately, their strategy was deceptive. Had they been willing to forsake their gods and follow the God of Abraham, Isaac and Jacob, the Lord would no doubt have withdrawn His hand of judgment, even if they were Canaanites. Rahab and her household illustrate this fact dramatically. But the Gibeonites did not allow their *accurate knowledge* to lead them to *proper actions*.

What was their strategy? And why was it so shrewd? The Gibeonites decided to deceive Israel by giving the impression that they had come from a far country, *outside* the land of Canaan. To accomplish their goal, they put on shabby clothes and sandals that would appear to be worn out from the long journey. Furthermore, they "took worn-out sacks on their donkeys, and wineskins, worn-out and torn and mended . . . and all the bread of their provision was dry and had become crumbled" (9:4,5). And when they arrived in Israel's camp, after traveling no more than 10 or 20 miles, "they went to Joshua . . . and said to him and to the men of Israel, 'We have come from a *far country*; now therefore, make a *covenant* with us' " (9:6).

But why was this so shrewd? The Gibeonite strategy actually involved a thorough knowledge of God's instructions to Israel long before they ever entered the land of Canaan. And they used this knowledge to deceive Israel.

And what was this knowledge? Many years before, God had said to Moses:

> *And I will fix your boundary from the Red Sea to the sea of the Philistines, and from the wilderness to the River Euphrates; for I will deliver the inhabitants of the land into your hand, and you will drive them out before you. You shall make no covenant with them or with their gods. They shall not live in your land, lest they make you sin against Me; for if you serve their gods, it will surely be a snare to you* (Exod. 23:31-33).

In other words, the Gibeonites knew specifically what God had said to Israel. No city in Canaan was to be spared—and *they* lived in Canaan. But they also knew something else—that God had made provisions to spare cities outside of Canaan. Moses made this very clear when he reviewed the law for Israel following their 40-year experience in the wilderness:

> *When you approach a city to fight against it, you shall offer it terms of peace. And it shall come about, if it agrees to make peace with you and opens to you, then it shall be that all the people who are found in it shall become your forced labor and shall serve you. However, if it does not make peace with you, but makes war against you, then you shall besiege it* (Deut. 20:10-12).

What God had said to Israel then helps explain the Gibeonite strategy. This is why they wanted to appear as if they had come from a "far country." Furthermore, they knew they had to make the first move. Rather than wait to be "made servants" they volunteered immediately to *be* servants (see 9:8). They knew they did not have the option to wait for Israel to approach them since they were Canaanites and had already come under God's judgment. Their solution was to try to convince Israel that they were from a distant place outside the land of Canaan.

Note too how shrewdly they avoided any reference to Jericho and Ai when they first approached Joshua:

> *Your servants have come from a very far country because of the fame of the Lord your God; for we have heard the report of Him and all that He did in Egypt, and all that He did to the two kings of the Amorites who were beyond the Jordan, to Sihon king of Heshbon and to Og king of Bashan who was at Ashtaroth* (Josh. 9:9,10).

Everything fit together perfectly. They had done their research well. In fact, they knew so much about Israel and their laws that it appears some of the people from Gibeon may have been "listening in" when Joshua reviewed the law of God at Mount Ebal and Mount Gerizim. They actually used God's instructions to Israel to reach their goal. They volunteered to be servants. They avoided any reference to Canaanite cities to give the impression they knew nothing of this land. Their clothes and their provisions were worn-out and appeared to be aged from traveling the long distance. And perhaps most impressive and deceptive, they acknowledged the God of Israel.

THE DECEPTION (Josh. 9:14,15)

The Gibeonite strategy worked in unbelievable fashion. Impressed with all the evidence, "Joshua made peace with them and made a covenant with them" (9: 15). Unfortunately he made this decision without seeking "the counsel of the Lord" (9:14). You see, there was another divine source God had given Israel for just such occasions. By going to the high priest Joshua could seek God's will directly regarding such matters (see Num. 27:18-21). But he didn't. Even though he had been skeptical earlier (see 9:7), he evidently became convinced that these people were telling him the truth. Unfortunately, he was deceived.

How could this have happened? The same as it can happen to anyone. Joshua was acting on the basis of what God had said his actions should be in circumstances such as this. The problem, however, was that the circumstances were not as Joshua thought they were. Consequently, he misapplied the Scriptures. He didn't have all the facts.

THE DISCOVERY (Josh. 9:16-22)

Ironically, it took only three days for Joshua to discover his mistake (see 9:16). Imagine Israel's surprise and chagrin when they heard that these people were neighbors. In order to make sure what they had heard was not a rumor, they traveled to their cities. After three days they arrived in Gibeon, the central location, and discovered three smaller suburban locations called Chephirah, Beeroth and Kiriath-jearim (see 9:17).

It was no rumor! Israel had been embarrassingly deceived. And because they had made a covenant with them in the *name* of "the Lord the God of Israel" there was nothing they could do to harm them. Even though Israel's mistake was based on false information, they had involved God—His name and His reputation—in their mistake. If they had broken their oath with the Gibeonites they would have brought the name of the Lord God of Israel into contempt among all the Canaanites. Though Israel definitely sinned in allowing themselves to be deceived, to break the covenant would have compounded the sin. Two wrongs never make a right.

THE CURSE (Josh. 9:23-27)

What was Joshua to do? He had violated the will of God by making a covenant with the Gibeonites. When he discovered his mistake he immediately demanded an explanation. "Why have you deceived us?" he asked (9:22). And at that point he could do only one thing— pronounce a curse of servanthood on the Gibeonites. "You shall *never cease being slaves*," he said (9:23).

Ironically, the Gibeonites were pleased with Joshua's decision. This is what they had anticipated and hoped for. They would rather serve Israel and *live* than to fight Israel and *die*. "We are in your hands," they responded to Joshua's indictment. "Do as it seems good and right in your sight to do to us" (9:25).

Though God had originally specified that the Gibeonites, like all Canaanites, were to be put to death, He honored Joshua's covenant to preserve them. Since His name was involved, He would not go back on His promise. And this God would demonstrate several times in behalf of these people.

The first time came soon after the covenant was

147

made. Five kings of the Amorites, angered and threatened by the Gibeonite strategy, decided to attack their cities (see 10:3,4). The Gibeonites, however, quickly sent word to Joshua asking for help. And Israel, because these people were now their servants by the covenant, acted immediately—and with God's blessing. In fact, on this occasion Joshua evidently sought the Lord's direct will through the high priest, for we read, "And the Lord said to Joshua, 'Do not fear them, for I have given them into your hands; not one of them shall stand before you'" (10:8). Again, Joshua learned a very valuable lesson.

LESSONS FOR TODAY

Perhaps the most significant lesson from this segment in Joshua's life is that Christians can be led astray by making superficial judgments based upon the Word of God. Remember that Joshua had just reviewed the complete law for Israel. They had spent days and perhaps weeks at Mount Ebal and Mount Gerizim. No doubt the statements God made regarding the fact that Israel could make a covenant with people outside of Canaan but not within Canaan were freshly embedded in Joshua's mind. And it was at this very point that Satan attacked this man of God and the other leaders in Israel and deceived them.

As we said at the beginning of this chapter, Satan is a subtle enemy, and lying is one of his common tactics. Jesus called him "the father of lies." And one of his most deceptive tactics is to use God's Word to achieve his insidious goals. In fact, Satan tried to lead Christ astray with this very strategy when he tempted Him in the wilderness. Taking Him to the pinnacle of the Temple, he said to Him, "If You are the Son of God throw Yourself down" and then, he said, "*for it is written*, He will give His angels charge concerning You; and on their

hands they will bear You up, lest You strike Your foot against a stone" (Matt. 4:6).

Christ of course was not deceived. He never was because He was the divine Son of God. In this case He reciprocated with the Word of God, *rightly interpreted and correctly spoken*, to counter Satan: "On the other hand," Jesus replied, "*it is written* 'You shall not tempt the Lord your God'" (Matt. 4:7).

How can a twentieth-century Christian fall prey to this kind of satanic tactic?

First, we can be deceived if we use the Bible "mystically." There are some Christians who take a very superficial and somewhat mystical approach in using the Word of God to determine God's will for their lives. For example, they allow the Bible to fall open, trusting that the first verse that meets their eyes will be God's specific word to them to help them make a particular decision.

No doubt, God can use this method, but it has many inherent dangers. And there is sufficient evidence that sincere Christians have been seriously led astray by using the Bible so superficially.

Second, we can be deceived if we read and study the Bible subjectively and without good principles of interpretation. This mistake in using the Bible to determine God's will is closely related to the first. However, it involves a more serious use of the Scriptures, often with the purpose of substantiating or proving a predetermined set of beliefs. In reality it is possible to make the Bible teach almost anything if we ignore the basic principles of literary interpretation. This kind of approach to Bible study has led to all kinds of erroneous systems of theology, which in turn have created a number of different cults and isms that deny the total truth of Scripture.

To understand the Bible and what God is actually saying to us today, we must remember to apply at least three basic principles:

- determine what the words, phrases and sentences of Scripture actually mean in context;
- discover what insights I can gain from the historical and cultural setting in which the Scriptures were written —what was the original meaning of scriptural statements;
- discern what grammatical, historical, cultural and literary reasons are there to take other than literal any statements in Scripture.

NOTE: Some people believe the Bible is allegorical and figurative, rather than an historical document containing normal literary techniques of allegory and figurative language to illustrate its literal meaning. This approach will lead to all kinds of false interpretations.

Third, we can be deceived if we bring circumstances to bear on Scripture rather than evaluating circumstances in the light of Scripture. Circumstantial factors *are* important in determining God's will. This we pointed out in the previous chapter. But we must never allow circumstances to be a *primary* factor in determining the Lord's will. They can be very deceptive, just as they were in Joshua's encounter with the Gibeonites. Everything looked so authentic, so right, so honest. And God had indeed spoken regarding what to do in this kind of situation. The problem was that the circumstances were not real.

It is at this point that Satan perhaps strikes the hardest. Since we live in a world of time and space, we become accustomed to evaluating events in the light of our circumstances. Consequently, Satan makes use of our natural tendencies, our cultural understanding and our psychological makeup.

At this juncture note too how fine the line is between making a correct decision and a very bad one. Had Joshua simply asked more questions, waited just a few days, and evaluated the total situation more carefully,

he would have discovered the deception before he made that final irreversible decision.

Fortunately, most of our mistakes are not irreversible. Some are. But most are not. And even in Joshua's case, he picked up the pieces and did what he could to correct the situation without committing a second sin to try to undo the first one. In Christ, there is always hope, no matter what our past mistakes.

LIFE RESPONSE

The fact that we have the Bible to guide us in making decisions is a great blessing. But we must make sure we use it correctly. Check yourself. Are you guilty of violating any of the following guidelines in your use of the Bible:

1. I tend to use the Bible mystically, in reality using a "spiritual chance" method in determining what God's will is for me personally.

2. I tend to read and study the Bible subjectively, violating basic principles of Bible interpretation, such as:

   a. Using a sound grammatical approach

   b. Considering the historical and cultural setting

   c. Taking God's Word literally unless there is sufficient reason to interpret it allegorically and figuratively.

3. I tend to allow circumstances to take precedence over God's Word in determining His will for my life.

FOLLOW-UP PROJECT

Memorize 2 Corinthians 11:14,15:

> *For even Satan disguises himself as an angel of light. Therefore it is not surprising if his servants also disguise themselves as servants of righteousness; whose end shall be according to their deeds.*

CALEB'S SPECIAL INHERITANCE

Caleb's Reminder (Josh. 14:6-9)
Caleb's Request (Josh. 14:10-12)
Caleb's Reward (Josh. 14:13-15)

One of the most difficult things for any Christian to do—yours truly included—is to be faithful in all things when we are not in a prominent position. Somehow we function better when others know how well we are doing.

This is a natural tendency. But the true test of our commitment to Jesus Christ and to His Body, the church, is how well we function when we have to operate behind the scenes, even making it possible for someone else to be in the limelight.

Caleb illustrates this kind of commitment as no other Bible character does.

Though the Bible says little about Caleb, what *is* written reflects a man who was Joshua's spiritual equal. In fact, in some respects, he excelled Joshua as a leader,

though once Joshua was appointed by God as Moses' successor, he stood quietly beside Joshua and often behind the scenes doing God's will in supporting the Lord's chosen leader of Israel.

Following Joshua's treaty with the Gibeonites, the events leading to the division of the land among the tribes of Israel are recorded in rapid succession.[1] The kings in southern Canaan were greatly threatened by the Gibeonites' alliance with Israel (see 10:1-5). Five of these men rallied their forces together and their first move was to attack the Gibeonites in order to punish them for joining Israel, and to keep Israel's strength from expanding even further. But the war was a fiasco for the kings of the south. Israel, because of their covenant with the Gibeonites, came to their rescue. They not only defeated the five kings, but one by one Israel defeated numerous other cities in southern Canaan (see 10:28-43).

Joshua then turned his attention to northern Canaan. The story is the same. God gave Israel one victory after another. There were no more Ai's and no more improper alliances. God was with Israel just as He said He would be if they obeyed His laws (see Josh. 1:8). Though it was a time-consuming process involving nearly seven years from the time they crossed Jordan (see 11:18), they defeated 31 kings in all (see 12:24). And then we read that "the land had rest from war" (11:23).

Understand, of course, that Israel had not captured all the Promised Land. In fact, "much of the land" remained "to be possessed" (13:1). But "Joshua was old and advanced in years" and consequently, God told him to stop doing battle and divide the land among the tribes of Israel (see 13:1,7). With their 31 victories, first in central Canaan with the fall of Jericho and Ai, followed by their southern and northern campaigns, Israel had broken the spirit of all remaining Canaanites (see map

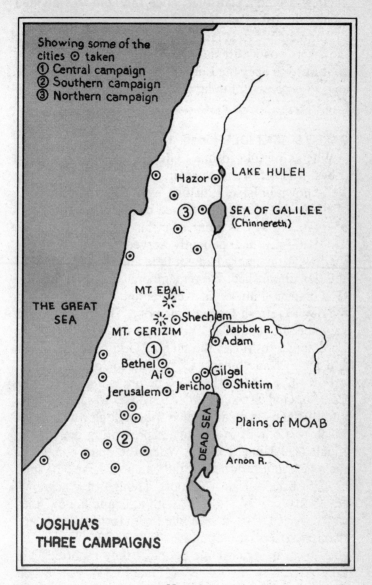

Showing some of the
cities ⊙ taken
① Central campaign
② Southern campaign
③ Northern campaign

LAKE HULEH

Hazor ⊙

③ ⊙ SEA OF GALILEE
(Chinnereth)

⊙

⊙ ⊙

MT. EBAL

☀

☀ ⊙ Shechem

MT. GERIZIM

Jabbok R.

⊙ Adam

THE GREAT
SEA

①

Bethel ⊙

Ai ⊙

⊙ Gilgal

Jerusalem ⊙ Jericho ⊙ ⊙ Shittim

⊙ ⊙

Plains of MOAB

⊙ ② ⊙

DEAD SEA

⊙ ⊙

Arnon R.

JOSHUA'S
THREE CAMPAIGNS

Map 4

155

4). It was God's plan that, once the land was divided among the tribes, each individual tribe was responsible to complete the task. Israel had been faithful to God and they were now entitled to their inheritance. And if they continued to obey the Lord, little by little they would be able to possess all the land God had promised to them (map 5).

CALEB'S REMINDER (Josh. 14:6-9)

When God told Joshua to divide the land among the tribes of Israel, we once again meet a man who is very well-known in Israel's history, even though in the book of Joshua he is only mentioned briefly. Though he was 85 years old at this moment in his life, and though he had faithfully and patiently served God in Joshua's shadow, his memory had not faded nor had his physical abilities diminished. He remembered a special promise God made to him 45 years earlier and he knew this was the day to refresh Joshua's memory. This he did with a very specific reminder: "You know the word which the Lord spoke to Moses the man of God concerning you and me in Kadesh-barnea," he said to Joshua (14:6).

Forty-five years earlier, long before Israel had entered Canaan, God issued an order to Moses to send 12 spies into the land—a man for each tribe. Along with Joshua, Caleb was one of those men, representing the tribe of Judah (see Num. 13:6,8). When the spies completed their task and returned to the camp of Israel, 10 spies brought back a negative report. Though they acknowledged that the land flowed "with milk and honey" they also reported it was a land filled with fortified cities and strong warriors (see Num. 13:27-29,32,33). "We are not able to go up against the people," they reported, "for they are too strong for us" (Num. 13:31). Fear begets fear and this negative report frightened the children of Israel.

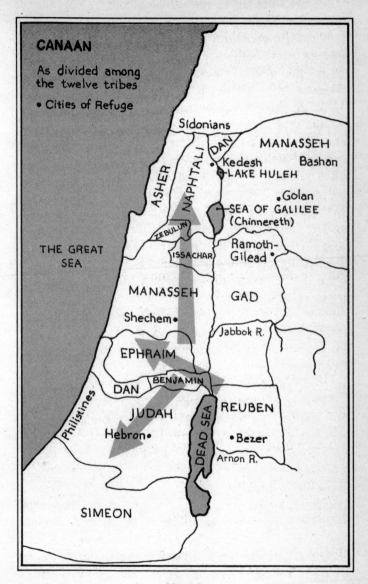

CANAAN

As divided among
the twelve tribes

• Cities of Refuge

Sidonians

DAN

MANASSEH

Kedesh

Bashan

LAKE HULEH

ASHER

NAPHTALI

Golan

SEA OF GALILEE
(Chinnereth)

ZEBULUN

THE GREAT
SEA

ISSACHAR

Ramoth-
Gilead

MANASSEH

GAD

Shechem

Jabbok R.

EPHRAIM

DAN

BENJAMIN

Philistines

REUBEN

JUDAH

DEAD SEA

Hebron

Bezer

Arnon R.

SIMEON

Map 5

157

But two of those 12 spies, Joshua and Caleb, thought differently. In the midst of a growing pessimism Caleb dared to disagree with the majority report. With great boldness and confidence in God's promises he "quieted the people before Moses," and shouted for all to hear, "We should by all means go up and take possession of it, for we shall surely overcome it" (Num. 13:30).

Note that at this moment Joshua was evidently silent. Though he agreed with Caleb, he remained in the background. Caleb was the spokesman. This computes with what we have already discovered about Joshua. In his earlier years he seemed to be reserved and in some instances a very fearful man, particularly when faced with leadership responsibility. Caleb appears to have been more courageous, bolder and more willing to face threatening situations head-on.

No doubt Joshua drew strength from Caleb's courageous behavior. When the fear generated by the spies evolved into anger and national rebellion against Moses, Joshua too took a frontal stand with Caleb and challenged Israel to claim God's promises and then to act on those promises:

> If the Lord is pleased with us, then He will bring us into this land, and give it to us ... only do not rebel against the Lord; and do not fear the people of the land, for they will be our prey. Their protection has been removed from them, and the Lord is with us; do not fear them (Num. 14:8,9).

Unfortunately, their exhortations and warnings went unheeded. The children of Israel threatened to stone Joshua and Caleb, which brought God's anger and wrath on them. Initially the Lord was going to destroy them all, right there and then. However, Moses succeeded in persuading Him to spare their lives. And once again God relented, but not without partial judgment. Because of their unbelief and failure to obey Him, God pronounced that all of that adult generation would never see the land. They would have to wander in the wilderness for 40 years until they died. Only their children would be able to enter Canaan.

But there were two exceptions—Joshua and Caleb (see Num. 14:38). Because of their willingness to obey God they would not die in the wilderness. They would be able to enter the land of Canaan.

But note that originally God singled out Caleb for this special blessing:

> Surely all the men . . . shall by no means see the land . . . But My servant Caleb, because he has had a different spirit and has followed Me fully, I will bring into the land which he entered, and his descendants shall take possession of it (Num. 14:22-24).

Why did God not mention Joshua's name at this moment? It seems that He was honoring Caleb for his initial courage and boldness. And because He would later honor Joshua as the new leader of Israel, He wanted all to know He would not forget Caleb. He was going to give him a *special inheritance* because he had followed the Lord fully (see Num. 14:14; Deut. 1:36).

And now 45 years later, when God instructed Joshua to divide the land among the tribes, Caleb stepped out of the shadows. He had waited many years for this moment. He remembered God's promise as if it were yesterday. And thus he reminded Joshua:

> I was forty years old when Moses the servant of the Lord sent me from Kadesh-barnea to spy out the land, and I brought word back to him as it was in my heart. Nevertheless my brethren who went up with me made the heart of the people melt with fear; but I followed the Lord my God fully (Josh. 14:7,8).

Though the biblical record in Numbers and Deuteronomy makes no reference to a *specific* inheritance for Caleb (only a general reference to the inheritance of the land), God must have mentioned at that time the exact area Caleb spied out in Canaan. Consequently, Caleb also reminded Joshua of Moses' response at that time to God's promise:

> *So Moses swore on that day, saying, "Surely the land on which your foot has trodden shall be an inheritance to you and to your children forever, because you have followed the Lord my God fully"* (14:9).

CALEB'S REQUEST (Josh. 14:10-12)

Following Caleb's reminder to Joshua, he then made his request. At age 85, after 45 years of faithful service to God since the promise was made, and after supporting Joshua in his leadership of Israel for seven war-filled years, he boldly and courageously asked for the "hill country about which the Lord spoke on that day" (14: 12). This specific request confirms the fact that the Lord had spelled out clearly that He would give Caleb a special place in Canaan because of his faithfulness.

The "hill country" was that area Caleb spied out many years before. And though it was strongly fortified and heavily populated by men of great size, God promised Caleb he would be able to defeat his enemies, even in his old age. And Caleb, at 85, was as confident of God's promise as he was in himself and his own abilities.

> *I am still as strong today as I was in the day Moses sent me; as my strength was then, so my strength is now, for war and for going out and coming in .... Perhaps the Lord will be with me, and I shall drive them out as the Lord has spoken* (14:11,12).

Here again we have that unique balance between

God-confidence and self-confidence so often illustrated in the Old Testament. And it should be noted that Caleb's use of the word "perhaps" does not imply doubt, but humility. Caleb *knew* he would win the battle. If he believed it when they were still in the wilderness 45 years before, how much more so now after having seen God deliver 31 Canaanite kings into their hands.

CALEB'S REWARD (Josh. 14:13-15)

Joshua remembered! How could he forget? He immediately blessed Caleb and gave him the land God had promised him for an inheritance. Perhaps his response went something like this: "Caleb, it's yours. You deserve it. I'm sorry I forgot! It is because of you that I mustered enough courage to take a stand against Israel's hostility and disobedience. It was because of you that I spoke out against their rebellion and unbelief. You helped me become the man that I am—a man that God could trust to lead Israel in place of Moses. I drew strength from you, Caleb. And you have been faithful to me. You've supported me, helped me, encouraged me. You never showed jealousy or resentment because you were not chosen to lead Israel—even though you were a stronger man than I, both physically and emotionally. I'm sorry I didn't remember God's promise myself. I'm glad you reminded me! It's yours! Take the mountain God promised you."

LESSONS FOR TODAY

Following are five very significant observations regarding Caleb's life, which in turn lead to five very practical twentieth-century lessons for every Christian.

First, three times in this passage it is stated that God's blessing on Caleb was based on the fact that he had "followed the Lord fully." God honored his faithful obedience to His commands.

161

God wants us to be obedient to *all* that He commands. Note however that the disobedience of Israel interfered with Caleb's desire to go into the land. Yet God viewed his true willingness to obey as actual obedience.

Sometimes twentieth-century Christians may be thwarted in their personal obedience because of group disobedience. Sometimes circumstances are beyond our control. In situations like this God looks at our hearts and what we do in the situation. Caleb was willing to take a stand for God's Word even though he knew he would be rejected by his own people. What about you?

WARNING: Christians must make sure they are taking a stand for *God's Word* and not for their own prejudiced opinions. Some Christians suffer needlessly because of lack of knowledge. In Caleb's case there was no question. Israel was in direct violation of God's command. In this situation Caleb would not compromise his convictions.

Second, Caleb's obedience was in the context of a minority report. The vote was 10 to 2 in favor of disobedience.

How easy it is to side with the majority; to compromise our Christian convictions; to operate out of fear. Not so with Caleb. Even when Joshua appears to have been afraid to speak up, Caleb spoke out boldly. What about you?

Third, Caleb's obedience was in the context of group rejection. The people literally wanted to stone him.

Fortunately, most of us have never had our lives threatened because of our stand for God's Word. However, it's easy to be inhibited and fearful even in the midst of minor rejections from those who do not want to follow God. The apostle Paul stands out as a dynamic example for all of us in this respect. "For I am not ashamed of the gospel," he wrote to the Romans, "for it is the power of God for salvation to every one who believes, to the Jew first and also to the Greek" (Rom. 1:16). And when he knew he was going to stand before the Roman emperor, perhaps to face the death penalty, he wrote to his faithful prayer supporters in Philippi:

> *For I know that this shall turn out for my deliverance through your prayers and the provision of the Spirit of Jesus Christ, according to my earnest expectation and hope, that I shall not be put to shame in anything, but that with all boldness, Christ shall even now, as always, be exalted in my body, whether by life or by death* (Phil. 1:19,20).

Fourth, Caleb's obedience continued for 45 years, even though Joshua was the man God chose to lead the children of Israel into the land.

How easy it is to become jealous and resentful when other Christians receive more attention than we do—especially when we feel we deserve it as much as they. To be faithful behind the scenes is difficult, but it is a true test of character. Remember, too, that God often tests us to see how faithful we are under these circumstances. If we pass the test, He then is able to entrust us with greater responsibility.

Fifth, Caleb's obedience was eventually honored and rewarded, even though it was 45 years later. God did not forget His promise to Caleb. He always honors faithful obedience.

Remember that God *never* forgets. Eventually He will reward all of us for faithful obedience. Like Caleb, some of that reward often comes in this life, but it will very definitely come in eternity. And of course, eternal rewards are those that really count.

LIFE RESPONSE

Select one of the following questions that applies to

you in a special way. Ask God to help you become a faithful and obedient Christian—to "follow the Lord fully" in all He says, no matter what the consequences to you personally. Write out a personal and specific goal that you want to carry out immediately—this week. Pray for God's help. Remember the words of Paul who said, "I can do all things through Him who strengthens me" (Phil. 4:13).

1. How obedient am I to all that God commands?

2. When the majority wants to do what is wrong in the sight of God, do I take a stand for what is right?

3. When I am faced with group rejection because I want to obey the Word of God, do I take a stand for what I know to be the will of God?

4. How faithful am I in my service to the Lord and to others when I have to work behind the scenes?

5. Am I willing to wait patiently for God to fulfill His promises to me?

FOLLOW-UP PROJECT

Memorize Matthew 10:42:

And whoever in the name of a disciple gives to one of these little ones even a cup of cold water to drink, truly I say to you he shall not lose his reward.

Note

1. Though numerous battles and victories are recorded in rapid sequence in the book of Joshua, it should be noted that the process involved a relatively lengthy period of time. It took approximately seven years from the time the children of Israel crossed Jordan and stepped onto the land of Canaan to win sufficient victories to break the military backbone of the Canaanites (see Josh. 11:18,23)

JOSHUA'S FINAL WORDS

A Short-range Perspective (Josh. 23)
A Long-range Perspective (Josh. 24)

One thing that has made a profound and fearful impression on my life is that I have observed men, whom God has mightily used, get sidetracked in their later years. The Bible itself is filled with illustrations of this kind—Solomon, for instance, and David, his father. Even God's great servant Moses failed God in his final days on earth, so much so that God could not let him lead the children of Israel into the Promised Land.

But there are exceptions. Joshua is one of those. Joshua stands out on the pages of the Old Testament as one of those rare biblical characters who consistently exemplified God's will and way throughout his lifetime. True, he was just as human as his fellow Israelites and at times he made some serious mistakes, but never as serious as those made by men who succeeded him as leaders in Israel. Though the reasons for his persistent and consistent faithfulness to God are rather vivid in his life story, nowhere are those reasons more clear than in his final words to Israel before he departed this life to enter the eternal presence of his heavenly Father.

Joshua's final exhortations to God's chosen people involved two historical perspectives following the division of the land among the tribes. The first perspective was *short-range*, including a review of God's faithfulness to Israel in the recent past, that is, since they had crossed over Jordan and experienced victory after victory in the land of Canaan. The second perspective was *long-range*, and included a review of God's faithfulness to Israel since God first chose and called Abraham out of an idolatrous environment in Ur of the Chaldees and graciously led him and his family into Canaan.

A SHORT-RANGE PERSPECTIVE (Josh. 23)

"Joshua was old, advanced in years" as he gathered Israel's leaders together to share with them the burden that lay on his heart (see 23:1). He had completed his earthly task. He had led Israel into the Promised Land. In seven years they had defeated the Canaanites sufficiently to eliminate any future military threat and resistance. He had just completed dividing the land among the tribes as God instructed. And now he had some final words, first about Israel's recent experiences in Canaan:
• "You have seen all that the *Lord your God* has done to all these nations because of you" (23:3a).
• "The *Lord your God* is He who has been fighting for you" (23:3b).
• "The *Lord your God*, He shall thrust them out from before you and drive them from before you" (23:5a).
• "You shall possess their land, just as the *Lord your God* promised you" (23:5b).
• "Cling to the *Lord your God*, as you have done to this day" (23:8).

166

- "For the *Lord* has driven out great and strong nations from before you" (23:9).
- "The *Lord your God* is He who fights for you" (23:10).
- "Take diligent heed to yourselves to love the *Lord your God*" (23:11).

Following this series of clear-cut and vivid reminders that it was no one else but the *Lord God of Israel* who had given them the land of Canaan, Joshua made his final point with equal clarity:

> *For if you ever go back and cling to the rest of these nations, these which remain among you, and intermarry with them, so that you associate with them and they with you, know with certainty that the Lord your God will not continue to drive these nations out from before you; but they shall be a snare and a trap to you, and a whip on your sides and thorns in your eyes, until you perish from off this good land which the Lord your God has given you (23:12,13).*

In summary, then, Joshua reminded Israel that it was the *Lord their God* who brought them into the land and gave them victory after victory. It was because of their love for Him and their obedience to do His laws that the Lord kept His promises to them. He had been faithful to them because of their faithfulness to Him. But should they forsake the Lord and begin to worship false gods, they would suffer the consequences, losing all they had possessed. "The anger of the Lord will burn against you," warned Joshua, "and you shall perish quickly from off the good land which He has given you" (23:16).

A LONG-RANGE PERSPECTIVE (Josh. 24)

Joshua's second and final address to Israel before he died at age 110 (24:29) was very similar in emphasis to his first address, but more comprehensive in terms of historical perspective. Furthermore, it was far more dramatic in terms of the geographical setting. Joshua "gathered all the tribes of Israel to Shechem"—a unique and significant place to deliver a farewell message. It was here (at Mount Gerizim and Mount Ebal) that Joshua built an altar to the Lord and wrote the law of God on large tablets of stones and reviewed these laws for all Israel (see Josh. 8:30-35).

But even more important, it was here in this very place that Abraham first received God's promise regarding the fact that He would give Israel the land of Canaan, and it was here Abraham demonstrated his rejection of the false gods by also building an altar to the Lord, the one true God (see Gen. 12:6,7).

But perhaps even more dramatic, it was also in this very place that Jacob, on his return from his carnal wanderings in Mesopotamia, cleansed and purified his own household from false gods by burying all his idols and likewise building an altar to the Lord (see Gen. 33:18-20; 35:1-4).

Again Joshua's primary concern for Israel is crystal clear. He wanted them to know that it was the God of Abraham, Isaac and Jacob who led them to this point in their history—not only in enabling them to do great exploits in Canaan since they crossed over Jordan, but right from the very beginning of their history. Thus Joshua quotes the Lord directly time and time again to make his point:

- "I [the Lord your God] took your father Abraham from beyond the River" (24:3).
- "I sent Moses and Aaron" to Egypt (24:5).
- "I brought your fathers out of Egypt" (24:6).
- "I brought you into the land of the Amorites . . . and I gave them into your hand" (24:8).
- "I delivered you from his [Balaam's] hand" (24:10).

- "I gave them [the Canaanites] into your hand" (24:11).
- "I sent the hornet before you" (24:12).
- "I gave you a land on which you had not labored" (24:13).

With this rapid series of quotations from the Lord Himself Joshua again culminated his address with an exhortation to Israel to "fear the Lord and serve Him in sincerity and truth" (24:14). He warned them to "put away the gods" which their fathers had served "beyond the River and in Egypt" and to "serve the Lord" (24:14).

Joshua then ended his formal address with what has become known as one of the most powerful and courageous testimonies and witness in all of Scripture. In his old and perhaps quavering voice, he shouted:

And if it is disagreeable in your sight to serve the Lord, choose for yourselves today whom you will serve: whether the gods which your fathers served which were beyond the River, or the Gods of the Amorites in whose land you are living; but for me and my house, we will serve the Lord (Josh. 24:15).

LESSONS FOR TODAY

Inherent in these two culminating messages to Israel lies the secret to Joshua's own success as a faithful and committed man of God. His final words reflect his personal philosophy of life and ministry. Several key observations grow out of these passages and become personal applications for *every* twentieth-century Christian and especially for *every* Christian leader.

First, Joshua believed that God was the only true God. Once Joshua turned from the gods of Egypt, he never forsook the one true God. Twelve times in chapter 23 Joshua referred to the "Lord your God" when reviewing the successes of Israel in the land of Canaan. This was a vivid reflection of who was first in his own life, for the Lord God of Israel was Joshua's Lord and God.

The true test of Joshua's commitment to God is reflected in his humility as he stood that day and addressed Israel. Looking back over the tremendous victories, how easy it would have been to exalt himself. After all, had not God said before they ever crossed Jordan, "This day I will begin to exalt you in the sight of all Israel!" (Josh. 3:7)? Joshua's statement to Israel at that time revealed his true perspective on himself and his relationship to God:

> *By this you shall know that the living God is among you, and that He will assuredly dispossess from before you the Canaanite, the Hittite, the Hivite, the Perizzite, the Girgashite, the Amorite, and the Jebusite .... [He is] the Lord of all the earth* (3:10,11).

And now, after God had fulfilled His promises, Joshua was still giving honor and glory to God. True, he realized full well that God had used him as a human instrument to achieve these goals. He did not apologize for the fact that God had used him to cut off these pagan nations and to yet assign the remaining nations as an inheritance for the tribes of Israel. He did not hesitate to say, "*I* have apportioned to you these nations" and "*I* have cut off" all the nations "from the Jordan even to the Great Sea toward the setting of the sun" (23:4). But Joshua also realized full well that it was God who had actually worked in behalf of Israel. Joshua was merely a human instrument utilizing the talents and abilities that God had given him.

This is a great example for every Christian living in the twentieth-century world. It is often easy to begin our Christian life giving glory to God. But as we grow older and as our own accomplishments increase, our natural tendency is to forget the source of our strength, our abilities, our achievements. How easy to exalt and honor ourselves—to even start serving "other gods," particularly the "god of materialism" or the "god of intellectualism." Like Joshua, we must realize that God *does* use our talents and our skills. Furthermore, material and intellectual accomplishments are not wrong in themselves. And it is not even wrong to use the word "I" to refer to our own efforts. But a Christian who puts God first in his life will always reflect with honesty and true humility that it is God who is responsible for all we are and have. The Christian who has a correct perspective on God's power and grace in his life can only agree with the apostle Paul who, sensing this very thing, wrote with great conviction:

> *Now to Him who is able to do exceeding abundantly beyond all that we ask or think, according to the power that works within us, to Him be the glory in the church and in Christ Jesus to all generations forever and ever. Amen* (Eph. 3:20,21).

Second, Joshua loved God with all his heart and soul. Putting God first in our lives and also loving Him are of course interrelated experiences. It follows naturally that if we truly believe that God is the *only true God*, we should then love and serve Him. The Lord Himself recognized this divine order when He gave the Ten Commandments. First He said, "You shall have no other gods before Me" (Exod. 20:3), and then He said, I will show "lovingkindness to thousands, to those who *love Me* and keep My commandments" (Exod. 20:6). From what we've seen in our study, Joshua followed this order in his own life and urged the children of Israel to do the same.

But what does it mean to love God? How is it expressed? These are very important questions, especially for today, since the word "love" is often defined as a purely emotional response. Not so in Scripture.

Joshua answered these questions clearly and specifically in a previous message to the Reubenites, the Gadites and the half-tribe of Manasseh—the tribes that dwelt beyond the Jordan River. Joshua warned:

> *Only be very careful to observe the commandment and the law which Moses the servant of the Lord commanded you, to love the Lord your God and walk in all His ways and keep His commandments and hold fast to Him and serve Him with all your heart and with all your soul* (Josh. 22:5).

Here indeed is a comprehensive definition of love for God. In short it means *total obedience*—doing what God says in every respect and with our total being—our minds, our hearts, our souls. Obviously, our emotions *are* involved. But obedience often means response to God's will whether we feel like it or not.

Joshua was this kind of man. The overall story of his life reflects obedience to the Lord in everything. And this is why he said unequivocally to Israel in his second farewell address, "Choose for yourselves today whom you will serve . . . but as for *me* and *my house*, we will serve the Lord" (24:15).

This statement was the culmination of a life lived in obedience to God's word. At the beginning of Joshua's career as Moses' successor in leading Israel, God said:

> *Be strong and very courageous, to be careful to do according to all the law which Moses My servant commanded you; do not turn from it to the right or to the left* (Josh. 1:7).

And now, years later, Joshua delivered his final words to Israel preceding his death, in essence using the very words God had spoken to him at the beginning of his career:

Be very firm, then, to keep and do all that is written in the book of the law of Moses, so that you may not turn aside from it to the right hand or to the left (23:6).

Joshua was faithful to God's original command. There were moments of course when he failed the Lord, such as when he was deceived by the Gibeonites. There were days when he was discouraged, such as when he failed to trust God following Israel's humiliating defeat at Ai. But the overall direction of his life was to obey God.

Joshua's love for God speaks to every twentieth-century Christian and also illustrates dramatically what Jesus taught His disciples. "He who has My commandments, and keeps them, he it is who loves Me," said Jesus. But, "He who does not love Me does not keep My words" (John 14:21,24).

Jesus emphasized the same thing to a lawyer who one day approached Him and asked a question: "Teacher, which is the great commandment in the Law?" Then Jesus answered: "You shall *love* the Lord your God with all your heart, and with all your soul, and with all your mind. This," said Jesus, "is the great and foremost commandment" (Matt. 22:36-38).

LIFE RESPONSE

1. To what extent do you really believe that God is the one true God? How is this reflected in your life? True, you may not be bowing down to idols of wood and stone. But what about the gods of materialism and intellectualism? The gods of sensualism? To what extent are you really honoring God above yourself?

2. To what extent do you love God? Is it with your whole heart and soul? What are your areas of disobedience? Do you realize that the degree to which you obey Him is the degree to which you love Him?

REMEMBER: love for God is *more* than feelings. It

173

involves commitment to Him no matter what our emotional response. It involves obedience to Him no matter what our personal desires. Love for God means obeying what He says even though it may hurt. Jesus demonstrated this love when He said in the garden: "My Father, if it is possible, let this cup pass from Me; yet not as I will, but as Thou wilt" (Matt. 26:39).

Evaluate your love for God. In which of the following areas do you believe your life needs the most attention? Pray that God will help you to improve in this area:

In your stewardship of time; that is, in the time you give to do His work;

In your stewardship of talent; that is, in the way you use your abilities and your skills to serve God;

In your stewardship of money; that is, in what you give to help others carry out His work;

In your stewardship of prayer; that is, in the time you give to praying about His work.

MEDITATION

*I want a principle within of watchful, godly
   fear,*
A sensibility of sin, a pain to feel it near.
*Help me the first approach to feel
   of pride or wrong desire,*
*To catch the wand'ring of my will,
   and quench the kindling fire.*

*From Thee that I no more may stray,
   no more Thy goodness grieve,*
*Grant me the filial awe, I pray,
   the tender conscience give.*
*Quick as the apple of an eye,
   O God, my conscience make!*
*Awake my soul when sin is nigh,
   and keep it still awake.*

Almighty God of truth and love,
*   to me Thy pow'r impart;*
The burden from my soul remove,
*   the hardness from my heart.*
O may the least omission
*   pain my reawakened soul,*
And drive me to that grace again,
*   which makes the wounded whole.*[1]

FOLLOW-UP PROJECT

Memorize Matthew 22:37,38:

> *And He said to him, "You shall love the Lord your God with all your heart, and with all your soul, and with all your mind." This is the great and foremost commandment.*

Note

1. Hymn, "I Want a Principle Within" by Charles Wesley.